Grace and Glory

The inspiring story of one small
church that reached out beyond its
walls to touch a community

Stephen & Julie Jonathan

O&U

Onwards & Upwards

Onwards and Upwards Publishers

3 Radfords Turf
Cranbrook
Exeter
EX5 7DX
United Kingdom
www.onwardsandupwards.org

First edition, published in the United Kingdom by Onwards and Upwards Publishers Ltd. (2019).

ISBN: 978-1-78815-748-3
Typeface: Sabon LT
Editor: Andrew Jonathan
Graphic design: LM Graphic Design

About the Authors

Stephen and Julie, originally from Swansea, South Wales, married in 1981, and have three adult children and two grandchildren. After working in local government, Stephen entered theological college as a mature student in 1984, and after three years of training joined the ministry team at City Church, Cardiff, as assistant pastor. During their time in Cardiff, they planted a new church on the outskirts of the city. Subsequently, Stephen was invited to become pastor of Tamworth Elim Church in 1992.

Julie, now retired, worked as a primary school teacher for many years and has always been actively involved in church life, serving especially with music and children's ministry. Since being in Tamworth, Stephen has gained Master's and Doctor's degrees in theology from Manchester and Bangor universities, respectively. His doctorate on the controversial subject of posthumous salvation was turned into a book, *Grace Beyond the Grave,* in 2014.

Julie and Stephen do their best to keep fit— Julie enjoys running and swimming and Stephen playing squash. Both also enjoy long walks. They are keen rugby supporters and are always ecstatic when Wales beats their arch rival England!

Endorsements

I have known Stephen as a friend since the first day we met in September 1984 as fledgling Bible College students. It was there I first saw Stephen's diligence, not only in searching for truth as a student of the scriptures, but also in seeking to serve God with a genuine love for people. Stephen records not just a fascinating account of some of the unique challenges and opportunities a local church pastor may face, but many helpful lessons that can inform and inspire others to believe that God can do something great with men and women who are willing to work with him in reaching those who are lost. I commend *Grace and Glory* to you as more than a narrative about church growth but a story of spiritual adventure, which like all great adventures has its fair share of both fear and faith.

Rev. Stuart Blount
Director of Ministry, Elim Pentecostal Churches

I have witnessed first-hand what has been achieved in and through Tamworth Elim Church. It's a fantastic example of God's generous justice at work in a local community. If you long to see God at work where you are, please read this book!

Rev. Lyndon Bowring
Executive Chairman of CARE;
Chancellor of Regents Theological College

This is the story of one local church told by the man who has for over 25 years pastored and led the many people who now call it home. From small and hesitant beginnings, over those years Stephen Jonathan has become a visionary leader and a champion of hope – hope for people and hope for the town and communities of Tamworth. Behind the inspirational headlines of the stories of growth, Stephen tells openly and honestly of the blood, sweat and tears along the way.

I am delighted Stephen has written this book. He is a rare breed – a thoughtful and disciplined scholar with a deep love for teaching God's Word. Yet, he is also a sleeves-rolled-up practical pastor and community leader. The *Grace and Glory* Stephen writes about is not mere theory to him. He has seen the evidence of that Grace in the lives of so many people who have come into contact with the love of God through the courageous and compassionate outreach of the church. I hope that many church leaders will read it and that many churches will begin to believe afresh for the transformation of their local community.

Rev. Chris Cartwright
General Superintendent, Elim Pentecostal Churches

Reading *Grace and Glory* reminded me of a quote from anthropologist Margaret Mead — "Never doubt that a small group of thoughtful, committed citizens can change the world; indeed, it's the only thing that ever has." This book is about the gracious actions of a church in a deprived area that opened its doors to anyone in need and cared for them. Stephen Jonathan has been brutally honest about the lows as well as the highs, the mistakes as well as the triumphs. He has made himself vulnerable in order to carry out God's work, and that comes with a personal cost. Together with his leadership team and congregation, Stephen has shown that Faith is sometimes spelled R-I-S-K as they have sought to change the world around them. An inspiring read.

Kathy Coe MBE
CEO Pathway Project — Action Against Domestic Violence

When Stephen Jonathan, an enthusiastic young Welsh pastor, arrived to head up Tamworth's Elim Church, he didn't know the town, the church or the myriad of challenges he would face. Over the next 25 years, as this excellent book reveals, Tamworth totally transformed him — and, more importantly, he helped transform Tamworth.

This well-written, challenging and very honest book charts Stephen's remarkable journey as he committed himself fully to making the church a key part of his local community. It will inspire anyone who realises the church is judged by the public on its works, as well as its faith.

Sam Holliday
Tamworth Herald Editor, 1999-2005

This book is interesting, inspiring and challenging for a wide range of readers. It will appeal primarily to the Tamworth Elim local church members as it tells the story of their own church's journey to move out beyond the walls of their church into the community around them. However, because it is the story of Stephen's own journey during his time of leadership in that local church, with some pastoral challenges and controversial theological issues, this will be attractive to a wider readership including existing pastors and those in training. The popular style of writing together with helpful reflections, plus the inclusion of a prayer after each chapter composed by Julie, make this a book to read and to recommend to others.

Dr Richard Massey
Former Principal of Birmingham Bible Institute /
Birmingham Christian College

As a former Mayor of Tamworth, I am immensely grateful for the work done by the Elim Church in Tamworth over the past thirty years. *Grace and Glory* tells the story of how thousands of lives have been touched by their work. By undertaking a wide variety of projects they have reached out, like Christ asked, to those at the crossroads and those on the by-ways.

Especially since the introduction of Austerity in 2010, they have provided a lifeline for the poorest in society who have been hardest hit. The Foodbank and the Winter Night Shelter have fed the hungry and sheltered the homeless when Universal Credit was piloted here. The night shelter involved working with all the other local Christian denominations, and provides a national model for community engagement as well as ecumenical co-operation.

Dr Simon Peaple
Labour and Co-operative councillor,
Leader of the Opposition on Tamworth Council,
and Roman Catholic social activist

Much has been written about church leadership, but in this moving story, Steve does so much more — he tells how it has worked in practice, in an ordinary English town with seemingly ordinary people. He writes with humility and honesty, with theological rigour and pastoral sensitivity, and Julie's beautiful prayers at the end of each chapter add so much to a book that really should be essential reading for anyone setting out in pastoral ministry.

Rev. Geoff Richardson
Former Dean of Students, Regents Theological College

As part of the leadership team at Tamworth Elim, I have walked alongside Steve and Julie for the past 20 years. This honest and heartfelt book captures (head, heart and soul) key lessons from the joys and struggles of leading a contemporary community church into the 21st century, by grace through faith.

Martin Wild
Author of *The Gospels in Harmony*

Acknowledgements

Without wishing to make this comparable to an Oscars awards speech, we feel that it would be improper not to give credit where credit is due.

Firstly, thanks be to God — Father, Son and Spirit — who is in the business of transforming lives and mending broken and damaged people. He is the One who takes a life and brings value and purpose to it. Just as he has done for us, we believe that he will do for others. Such gracious transforming power provides us with faith, hope and love.

Secondly, we wish to thank our church family for their love and support for well over a quarter of a century. It has been a wonderful, wonderful journey together and better than we could ever have hoped. Special commendation is deserved to those who attended Tamworth Elim at the start of our ministry and who have "persevered" with us for the entire journey: Dave and Corine, Brian and Carol, Siân, Jan, Maureen, Paul and Sharon, Margaret J, Bev, Margaret and Tony, Brian P, Sue R, and Tim and Deb.

Thirdly, a big "thank you" to all who have served alongside us as part of our church leadership team throughout the years. Some have come and others gone during this time, but the overarching vision of community transformation has persisted. It is a real privilege working together with our present team: Dan, Brenda, Fiona, James, Nick, Tim and Martin.

Fourthly, we are so privileged to have such great endorsements from such talented practitioners from the world of theology, journalism, politics, church leadership at national and local levels, education and community engagement. Thank you for your kind words and support. We would also like to thank our son, Andrew, who has a sharp eye for detail, for copy-editing the transcript. We think that he found a kind of perverse pleasure in pointing out the mistakes of his parents! So appreciated, Andy!

Finally, we would like to thank Luke Jeffery and the staff of Onwards and Upwards for their help and assistance in bringing *Grace and Glory* to completion.

Dedication

To the many unsung heroes at Tamworth Elim Church —
most of whom have not been mentioned by name in this book —
who have faithfully served the purposes of God
quietly and without acclaim.
"...your Father who sees what is done in secret will reward you."
(Matthew 6:4)

– & –

To our three wonderful children,
David, Siân and Andrew,
all blessed with a heart for the marginalised.

– & –

To our delightful grandchildren,
Amélie and Elijah,
who bring such joy and gladness to Mamgu and Grandad.
Thank you for your love.

Contents

Foreword...13

Preface 15

1. Early Days in Ministry 19
2. Moving to the Midlands............................23
3. Getting Settled 28
4. Getting Started 33
5. What is in Your Hand? 37
6. Our First Community Project 41
7. Expanding the Team 46
8. More than a Building Project...................49
9. Making Maximum Impact 60
10. Days of Forming, Days of Filling............69
11. Man Plans and God Laughs! 77
12. Outgrowing Our Facilities.......................86
13. Becoming Foolish for Christ 92
14. Lottery Funding 98
15. Our Day in Court.....................................106
16. New Buildings, New Opportunities 112
17. The Tough Years (1) 119
18. The Tough Years (2) 126
19. Better Times...135
20. Changing of the Guard.............................145
21. Money, Money, Money!.............................153
22. Grace – Our Greatest Motivation 162
23. Acts 29 173

Contact the Authors 176

Grace and Glory

Foreword

Grace and Glory is an important book for several groups of people.

The people who will find it of immediate interest are those who belong to the Tamworth Elim Church. It's their story. A story of a church that learnt to engage with their wider community in a way that was a blessing as they demonstrated all the implications of the gospel.

For those of us who listen in to their story, we are reminded that the gospel is always made particular. It's lived out by a particular group of people in a particular place at a particular time. In the same way that all families need to keep hold of their own personal stories, I believe strongly that all churches need to be able to learn how to tell their story. Reading this account might help others record their own story of how God has been involved in and through their church community.

The next group who will find this of significance are people who are interested in the theology and practice of Pentecostal churches.

Reflecting on his decades of being a Pentecostal pastor, Stephen reminds us of how British Pentecostalism changed over the last quarter of the twentieth century. The church in Tamworth is almost a perfect example of those changes. From being a small, somewhat inward-looking congregation, meeting in a tin hut, it grew to own multipurpose buildings that engaged with some of the town's most difficult-to-reach people. And that happened, in large part, due to the entrepreneurial leadership of a young pastor who knew that his church could see more than they had ever imagined.

Intriguingly, it also offers a chance to hear how Pentecostals reflected on a breadth of doctrinal positions that at times proved uncomfortable for all concerned. Doctrinal positions do matter, but they do change and develop. Classical Pentecostals have had a doctrinal certainty of the order of events that should happen to all Christians. For working pastors to challenge that is initially disconcerting, but ultimately healthy. For a denomination to be mature enough to recognise that emphases may differ, even as the expectation of the dynamism of the Spirit remains, enables honesty and growth in everyone.

Finally, this is an important book for anyone interested in "ordinary theology" and specifically "ordinary ecclesiology" at the end of the twentieth century and in the first decades of the twenty-first. This is lived theology and lived practice. Imagine how thrilled we would be to discover a local pastor's reflection on life in a local congregation in Ephesus in the year 150. Or Dublin in 850. Or a village outside Geneva in 1530. Or London in 1750. Or Nairobi in 1930.

This was Tamworth in 2019.

Who knows whether we will have another 500 years or so on planet Earth before Jesus transforms everything. But if we do, I love to think that one day someone will find this book tucked away in a dusty storage box and will read about all the extraordinary things that God did in an ordinary church with ordinary people in an ordinary place.

And people will probably be so encouraged to read of all that was written here.

You don't have to wait that long. You can turn the page and begin now. But just keep remembering, what you are reading is church history. And the purpose of all history is to encourage us to embrace all that God could do in our own day.

Enjoy this important book.

Dr Neil Hudson
Church Consultant (LICC) and Elim Pastor
Author of *Imagine Church*

Preface

One lazy Saturday afternoon in early April, Julie and I sat by the River
Avon having earlier walked around the town of Stratford, the quaint
birthplace of the bard himself, William Shakespeare. We had just enjoyed
a cream tea and a leisurely browse around second-hand bookshops,
which is a favourite pastime for many visitors to this lovely Warwickshire
town. We are always on the look-out for a bargain buy, and enjoy the
sense of wellbeing in knowing that our purchase is going to help some
local charity raise much-needed funds. Julie, as ever, focused on the
fiction and children's education sections, as a former school-teacher who
now has our grandchildren's educational advancement in mind in
addition to a good holiday read. For me, as with most pastors I know, it
is the theology and religion sections that captivate my attention. I'm
always on the lookout for a title from one of my favourite authors at a
bargain price. If the truth be told, these days I probably give more books
away to young leaders and those enquiring after the faith that has
transformed my life, than I purchase for myself. Having said that, old
habits die hard! As with many pastors of my age, fast approaching my
sixtieth birthday, I have accumulated a sizeable library. I must say that I
was a late starter and had not read a theological book — to be honest,
any books at all — until I was 25 years old. My life has dramatically
changed since then, and books have become not only the tools of my
trade, but also a joy to me.

Where was I? Oh yes, Julie and I were sitting by the River Avon,
enjoying watching the boats pass by, with little children waving to
everyone in the hope of a response, dog-walkers with their prized pets
unleashed, and older folk enjoying the opportunity to get some fresh air
following the recent cold spell. We love these times as it provides us with
opportunity to chat about our family, our lives, church matters, and
reminisce over our youth — we started dating when we were teenagers,
not that many people use the word "dating" these days. Showing my age
now!

It was on this occasion that I was reminded of a conversation a few
months earlier with Chris Cartwright, the General Superintendent of the
Elim Church, the Movement to which I belong, urging me to write about

how God has used our small church in Tamworth to touch the lives of thousands of local people, in a variety of ways. As far as I remember, I was quite resistant to Chris's encouragement to write, stating that I was too busy getting on with "doing" church to be taking time out to write about it. I do hope that my response to Chris was a little more gracious than it appears in script! Chris, however, was insistent that I give this some further thought as he believed that our story might offer some inspiration, encouragement and even instruction on how God can use a small church such as ours. I had shelved that conversation until that lazy Saturday afternoon in Stratford as I watched the world go by.

I have previously authored a book which was of a more academic nature, based on my doctorate in theology some years back. I had hoped to write again someday, maybe in retirement, on some gritty theological issue, but not the kind of book that *Grace and Glory* has turned out to be.

Grace and Glory would find itself most definitely in the religion/ theology section in those second-hand bookshops in Stratford, but would be much more difficult to categorise in a more specialist library of a university or theological college. *Grace and Glory* is a book about a church, Tamworth Elim Church, but is not just a church biography merely replaying stories of faith and blessing, though it does contain many exciting stories of bold faith in its pages. It is not an autobiography of my ministry, though admittedly there are autobiographical aspects to it. It is not a theology of the church, though both theology and church appear significantly in the script as it has always been my view that one's theology affects one's practice; we need to look no further than to Paul's letters to Romans and Ephesians to see that belief precedes behaviour. *Grace and Glory* does not focus on biblical studies and exposition, but you will find many references to scriptural teaching underpinning our ministry values and vision.

To borrow Bill Hybels' now famous maxim, "The local church is the hope of the world." I would suggest that *Grace and Glory* is about one local church attempting to bring hope to a market town in south east Staffordshire, in the English Midlands. It is a story of the 25-year journey of a small church reaching out to its community, armed with love and hope, truth and compassion, touching the lives of thousands of people. It is a story about God using rather weak and foolish people who dare to trust his leading, emphasising spiritual principles and New Testament values which are worked out in day-to-day living.

This book focuses on the narrative of Tamworth Elim Church over a quarter of a century and its inspiring story of community transformation. During this time our gracious God opened many doors for us to walk through. The name Elim is taken from Exodus 15:27 and tells of the children of Israel walking around in the desert of Sinai, parched and in need of refreshment and shade. It was at this time they came across an oasis called Elim, with seventy stately palm trees offering shade from the sun and cool, refreshing water. Tamworth Elim Church seeks to be that oasis to people today, offering support and shelter, encouragement and inspiration, guidance into a better way, and hope for the future to those who are bruised by life's struggles and turmoil.

This is a tale of God at work. Whilst we can tell of significant building projects, a host of new community outreaches, a church congregation that has been blessed by over 400% increase, and many lives transformed by the power of the gospel, the real hero of the story is none other than God himself. To be entirely truthful, which is always a good thing to be, none of what you are about to read is the result of some wonderfully creative church leader or leaders, because all we were doing was thinking God's thoughts after him. There has been many a time we seemed to trip over something and then realised that the Lord was the one doing the tripping!

Like many churches, we have our maxims and mottos, but I want to take some time to unravel the rationale and spiritual principles behind the statements. I would hate it for you to just take away the words without the heart, which could amount to some kind of gimmickry or "spiritual spin".

But why *Grace and Glory?* Quite simply, these two words capture the heart of the Christian journey, which is all by God's Grace and ultimately for God's Glory. God owes us nothing, yet we are beneficiaries of his amazing grace, a love that we do not deserve and cannot earn. Every success and every "win" is for the honour and glory of God. It is he, and he alone, who deserves praise and honour.

Grace and Glory will hopefully inspire, encourage, inform and possibly on occasions provoke. It will remind us that God continues to use weak and foolish people to be his partners in mission, and that he continues in the work of transforming lives and communities in our day. Whilst the narrative of this book has been written by me, I want to thank Julie for her participation in aiding my memory, editing the script, and for concluding each chapter with a prayer. During the writing, there were occasions when we both chuckled with delight as we recalled comical moments, and other instances when we simply sat awestruck over God's amazing grace to us. I am blessed beyond measure by Julie's love, friendship and partnership in the gospel throughout our married lives, as well as her important contribution to this book.

We have been thrilled, humbled and amazed that God has used us, and quite overwhelmed that some people, unconnected to our church community, have encouraged me to share our story more widely in the belief that it will stimulate the faith of others. Indeed, it is my prayer that in some small way these pages will serve the purposes of God through encouraging our fellow Christians to see that all things are possible with God.

Dr Stephen Jonathan (2019)

CHAPTER ONE

Early Days in Ministry

FOLLOWING THE YEARS OF THEOLOGICAL AND MINISTERIAL training at Elim Bible College in the mid-1980s, I served as an assistant pastor in a city centre church of about 500 people, in Cardiff, the capital city of Wales. This was a rather scary step up from theological college to pastor people who were generally more spiritual, more experienced and more intelligent than me. It was a sharp learning curve, and as I look back I cringe with embarrassment over my lack of wisdom in some pastoral situations. Thirty years on, I acknowledge that I still have my "L" plates on, and continue to be occasionally less than wise; having said that, it is an evidence of God's grace that he should have used this young guy in his late 20s, or indeed the older version of him, to achieve anything for his kingdom's purposes. I continue to be challenged by the truth of Paul's words to the Corinthian Christians, that God has chosen the weak and foolish things of this world to shame the strong and wise (1 Cor. 1:27) and that God has his treasure in jars of clay (2 Cor. 4:7). An amazing paradox — the total sufficiency of God is revealed through the insufficiency of humans. Who, other than God, could have ever thought of that?!

During my third year in that city centre church, Julie and I had the opportunity to start a church in a new residential estate on the outskirts of the city. If the city centre church had been a learning curve, this next step was simply off the scale in my pastoral "education". The new estate had been built as an extension to a rather well-to-do suburb of Cardiff, and was designed to receive many of the families rehoused from the redeveloped docks areas of the city. The three years spent in establishing a church in such a disadvantaged community was an eye-opener in every sense of the word. The estate, in the late 1980s and early 1990s, was renowned for its social challenges. Yet, it is my belief that this is exactly where the church is meant to be!

A favourite piece of prose of mine is written by George MacLeod:

I simply argue that the Cross be raised again
At the centre of the marketplace
As well as on the steeple of the church.
I am recovering the claim that Jesus was not crucified
In a cathedral between two candles;
But on a Cross between two thieves: on a town garbage heap;
At a crossroad of politics so cosmopolitan
        that they had to write
His title in Hebrew and in Latin and in Greek.
And at the kind of place where cynics talk smut,
        and thieves curse and soldiers gamble.
Because that is where He died, and that is what He died about
And that is where Christ's men ought to be,
And what church people ought to be about.[1]

The three years spent in that place would provide more than enough subject matter for a book of its own. The outreach touched the lives of many people on the margins of society, those who could never be thought of as your average churchgoers — an understatement if there ever was one! For example, there were those who used expletives in the middle of their prayers as they declared their praises to the God who had changed their lives — "God I think you are ******* wonderful," said one man, with another heartily responding with an "Amen!" to the sentiment just paid to the Almighty. There was the guy who had a new tattoo of the face of Jesus to proclaim his new-found allegiance, which sounds surprisingly normal some thirty or so years later in a society where it appears the minority has chosen not to be on the receiving end of a tattooist's needle. Then there was George (not his real name), a demonised guy who was given a "mission" to kill the pastor! Yes, those stories are true, plus another barge-load of them! Sharing communion was also interesting as it was not always easy to direct one's thoughts on the Cross when local teenagers firmly placed their naked buttocks against the windows of the building where the church met.

---

[1] MacLeod, George, *Daily Readings with George MacLeod,* Glasgow, Wild Goose Publications, 2001, 106.

One evening, the school caretaker, who had arrived to close the school following our meeting, made some very derogatory remarks about some of the people that we had in our church at that time — people with learning disabilities and those who were on the margins of society — though the man didn't phrase his observations quite as politely as I just did. "Your church seems to attract them!" he said sneeringly. He was not only disparaging the people, but also belittling the work our new church was attempting to undertake on this new housing estate.

I responded, "Society turns such people away. Their reaction is just like yours, but the reason that we gather people that you would call odd, is that they know that in our church they will find love and acceptance. The world at large might pile them on the garbage heap, but we don't. They are precious to us because they are precious to God."

He was a tough guy yet walked away with tears in his eyes. I have no idea why that remark touched something quite deeply within him, or what God was beginning to do in his heart at that time, but it was one of those occasions when I sensed God providing me with an answer that was well beyond my own wisdom.

There is an interesting exchange of letters between a second century Greek historian, Celsus, an opponent of Christianity, and a church leader named Origen.

Celsus wrote, "When most teachers go forth to teach, they cry, 'Come to me, you who are clean and worthy,' and they are followed by the highest calibre of people available. But your silly master cries, 'Come to me, you who are down and beaten by life,' and so he accumulates around him the rag, tag and bobtail of humanity."

Origen replied, "Yes, they are the rag, tag and bobtail of humanity. But Jesus does not leave them that way. Out of the material you would have thrown away as useless, he fashions men, giving them back their self-respect, enabling them to stand on their feet and look God in the eyes. They were cowed, cringing, broken things. But the Son has set them free."[2]

I thank God that he has a passion for the lost, the least and the lonely — a passion that impassions me.

---

[2] Cited by Arthur John Buttrick, *The Interpreter's Bible: Luke, John,* New York, Abingdon-Cokesbury Press, 1951, 603.

Dear God,

Thank you for loving us so completely, just as we are, the rag, tag and bobtail of humanity. We are enormously grateful that you don't leave us that way, but change us to become more like Jesus.

Lord, help us not to hinder that process, but allow you to change those things in our lives that displease you and are less than helpful to our fellow life travellers and for our own well-being. Please help us to see ourselves and others through your eyes, so that we don't distort truth — the truth that says that we're all equal; the truth that states that we are all loved by you and precious in your sight.

Help us when we are tempted to feel superior to remember that we are what we are by your grace; and as we revel in your boundless grace, may we be filled with compassion for those around us, and serve them cheerfully, for we know that in doing so, we serve and worship you.

Amen.

CHAPTER TWO

Moving to the Midlands

FIVE YEARS AFTER THEOLOGICAL COLLEGE, LIFE WAS ABOUT to change for our young family. We had come to a place where our ministry in South Wales was ending. How did we know? We just did, and didn't like it very much. I am often suspicious of people who seem to hear from God so clearly and easily, whether it is to move church, move house or which supermarket to shop in this week. For me, I struggle to hear God's voice quite that clearly, and certainly over something as important as leaving a church that I had given my life and soul to for the previous three years. It wasn't just moving church, but moving home, moving our children from their schools, moving away from our friends, moving further away from our immediate family. There was no way that Julie and I could be nonchalant or blasé over such a decision. We had only moved into our home 18 months previously and had a five-year plan to decorate and refurbish. Besides all that, Julie didn't want to live across the border as a "missionary" to the English any more than I did!

As much as we desired to stay and work with our new church, we felt that the doors were closing on our ministry there. Church-planting is hard, and in some places it is harder than others. Our estate was one of those places. I remember that on one occasion close to the end of our ministry there, I asked Julie to speak on a Sunday. I simply had nothing left to give or to say. Now, for many pastors' wives, speaking on a Sunday is no big deal, but it was for Julie. Julie, although articulate and able, simply didn't do sermons. Yet, on this occasion she did, as my tank was empty and it wasn't a comfortable place to be.

Being a part of a denomination has its benefits and one of them was being invited to consider another church, a new start, a fresh page, turning over a new leaf. We were invited to consider the Elim Church in Tamworth. We were aware of this town, and this church, as it was the church that two of our friends at theological college had attended. To cut

23

a long story short, we went through the interview process of talking with the eldership, with whom we were very impressed. They were an easy-going, forward-thinking team, mainly in their thirties.

We weren't expecting some writing in the sky or a voice from heaven, or even a verse to jump off the pages of the Bible instructing us to go to Tamworth. Please don't bother looking up Tamworth in a concordance; it isn't there! I've looked! We might not have expected such a clear communication from heaven, but we were expecting a deep peace about the rightness or wrongness of such a move. It didn't come. Or, it might have come and we missed it, a bit like Thomas who was out buying the *Jerusalem Mail* when Jesus called around for tea! Don't look for that in a concordance either! The result was, we remained uncertain about whether we were to move to the English Midlands or not. We had, some years previously, given up home, jobs and proximity to family and friends to go to theological college with our young children, so this wasn't beyond us. The difference was this: on previous occasion we were pretty confident that that was what God wanted of us, and as we'd heard many times from pulpits, the best place to be is in the centre of God's will for our lives. It is a statement with which we wholeheartedly agree and if God wanted us to move to the Midlands, then we would do it, but we didn't really know what he wanted.

The Tamworth church leaders weren't any more clued in to the Father's will than we were as they also remained unsure of this young couple from over the border. We were invited up for a weekend at the church, and invited to speak at a Sunday service. This wasn't "preaching with a view" as some churches practise, at least that wasn't the way we understood the weekend. It was just an opportunity to get to know each other a little better. It seemed like practical good sense to one and all.

Even after the weekend visit, the Lord still didn't provide us with a clear directive of whether this was a match made in heaven or not. We didn't get a "man from Macedonia" appear to us in a dream, instructing us to "come to Tamworth", but somehow it happened. Read Acts 16 if you have no idea what I am talking about. Since there was such indecision on both sides, Julie and I assumed that it would do for now, and that the Lord would open another door on a later occasion — the place where he *really* wanted us to be. But since the door was clearly closing on our church plant ministry in South Wales, and this appeared to be the only other door which seemed at least partly open, then we would walk through it — yet we remained quite unconvinced. As I said previously, I don't always find it easy to hear God's voice with clarity.

Our story reminds me of Fr. John Kavanaugh, a university lecturer who spent a year in India to focus on prayer, service and ministry to the poor, and a month in Calcutta, at Mother Teresa's House of the Dying. At that time John was seeking a clear answer as to what to do with the rest of his life, and whether he should return to the United States and become a philosophy professor or continue to work with the poor in India or Africa. On the first morning in Calcutta, he met Mother Teresa.

She asked him, "What can I do for you?"

John asked her if she would pray for him.

"What do you want me to pray for?" she asked.

He requested that she pray for him to have clarity so that he would know what to do with his life.

She stated rather firmly that she would not do that. When he asked her why she would not pray for clarity, she responded with, "Clarity is the last thing that you are clinging to and the thing of which you need to let go." John was rather puzzled by this reply and stated that she seemed to have the clarity he so longed for, at which point she laughed and said, "I have never had clarity; what I have always had is trust. So I will pray that you will trust God."[3]

Having read that story, I felt much more at ease. If lack of clarity was OK for Mother Teresa, then it is OK for me. To tell you the truth, there have been many times when I have prayed for clarity to know God's will and for God to reveal his plan and purposes so that I might walk obediently where he desires. Maybe I should pray for clarity less and for trust more? The scriptural principle found in Proverbs 3:5,6, "Trust in the Lord with all your heart and lean not on your own understanding; in all your ways submit to him, and he will make your paths straight," reveals to us that the Lord promises to make our paths straight as we choose to trust him and follow his ways, but doesn't promise to tell us *how* he is going to direct our paths. The promise is for direction, not necessarily for clarity.

Over the years, as I have reflected upon the devastation and death of so many innocent people through acts of terrorism and through catastro-

---

[3] Walls, J. L., Neill, J., and Baggett, D., eds., *Venus and Virtue: Celebrating Sex and Seeking Sanctification,* Eugene, OR., Wipf and Stock Publishers, 2018, 207.

phic incidents, I find myself asking for clarity. *Why Lord? Couldn't you have stopped that? Were you unable or unwilling? Why allow such suffering and misery if you had the power to prevent it? You only needed to say, "Be still!" as you did to the storm on Lake Galilee.* Then I lower my voice and realise that in the midst of my confusion and craving for clarity, God is God and I am not! I've been a follower of Jesus now for over 40 years, and the hard questions don't go away. In some senses, I have more questions, different questions, than I had at first. As I look back, I would confess that 25 years ago I knew more than I confess to knowing now. Please don't misunderstand, as I'm not saying that I have forgotten the things that I knew back then or have had a serious case of memory loss. No! Rather, back then, my faith was more doctrinaire, more mechanistic. It had fewer loose threads and more slick answers. In fact, I think I had an answer for most things! Now, not so! I am much more content with mystery and the transcendence of God, and I don't feel the need to provide a watertight argument for God's dealings with his creation any more.

I love the quote from Bishop Kallistos Ware, a revered Eastern Orthodox theologian, in his book *The Orthodox Way.* He writes, "It is not the task of Christianity to provide easy answers to every question, but to make us progressively aware of mystery. God is not so much an object of our knowledge as the cause of our wonder."[4]

Clarity is over-rated! Trust is better! And maybe the best approach to life's mysteries is found in a song a friend of mine once wrote, "Teach me to trust your ways, O Lord; your ways are so much higher than mine."

God must laugh at our attempts to second-guess his plan for our lives at times. Julie and I had worked it out — or so we thought, the rational beings that we are — that God didn't want us to stay around in Tamworth that long, as we didn't receive a clear "call" from God, and that our true calling would come in due course. Twenty-six years on, we're still here, and as we reflect on God's gracious dealings with us, we continue to be amazed.

What a faithful God have I,
What a faithful God,

---

[4] Ware, K., *The Orthodox Way*, New York, St. Vladimir's Seminary Press, 1979.

What a faithful God have I,
Faithful in every way.

Dear Lord,

We are so prone to feeling like we're in a muddle. Even when our hearts are in the right place and we desire to do your will, we can get confused. That confusion leads to frustration and impatience. We long to hear your voice, but sometimes you remain silent, or maybe we don't listen attentively enough. Either way, in those times, Lord, help us to trust you.

We know that you have never let us down, and your promise to "never leave us nor forsake us" still stands. Thank you! Whatever our circumstances, we choose to put our hands in yours, and are assured that you will lovingly, faithfully, gently guide us.

Amen.

CHAPTER THREE

Getting Settled

Taffs among the Tammies!

WE SETTLED IN A WONDERFUL NEW HOME, JUST A FEW minutes' walk from the church. Not exactly living above the shop, but close enough to be on hand should we need to be. The children, then aged ten, eight and six, settled easily into their new school and were objects of fascination to their new friends, due to their accents more than anything else.

The church had experienced significant losses over the previous decade, largely due to differing views on charismatic renewal and leadership styles. To be truthful, I was quietly thanking God that those battles had already been fought before I arrived. Those who remained were not up for infighting over churchy squabbles and theological hair-splitting. Having said that, I am very aware of how difficult life must have been for my predecessors. The church we inherited in 1992 was about 55 strong on a good day. The congregation met for worship on a Sunday morning, had four house groups, a Thursday evening children's club, and a "mums and tots" group which was in the process of closing down. It appeared that few visitors ever attended our church on a Sunday, and I wasn't that surprised. The building, although only 15 years old, was erected in place of the former building which had been knocked down following a Compulsory Purchase Order being actioned by the county council highways department. The council intended to widen the main road leading to the town centre, and then changed its mind. The new building was uninviting and stylistically bland. Prince Charles would have had a field day in berating its architecture. When Julie and I first visited the place, I asked her what she thought of the building. Her reply was, "It looks like a bloomin' air-raid shelter!" I guess that she wasn't too impressed either.

Whatever the ambience and aesthetics of the building, or not, it was certainly an improvement on our previous experience of not having a building at all. In our church plant in South Wales, we needed to clear the space, often mop the floors from beer spills the previous evening, collect the piano from a church member's home on the estate, set up the PA system, chairs and banners, take down the sexual health posters and exhibits from the walls, as we didn't want to offend the Almighty or, for that matter, the dear elderly ladies who had started coming to our church. At least, in Tamworth, the church was clean and chairs were set out. The PA was someone else's job. Praise God for small mercies. The other difference was that most of the congregation in Tamworth owned cars, which was not the case in the church plant, where I provided a shuttle service of carrying and fetching church items and elderly people from outlying parts of the estate for up to an hour before the service started. Church-planting isn't for wimps! As insubstantial as the facilities were in Tamworth, they seemed a luxury by comparison.

Following the spiritual war zone of church-planting, we enjoyed the relatively stress-free "honeymoon" period pastoring in a suburb of this white, working-class town. The leaders were wonderfully supportive and many people were open for God to do a new thing amongst us. The former pastor had even declared that he was not the man to lead the church into its future and prophesied that the new pastor would be a man with the keys to unlock the doors of blessing. No pressure there then! I am so glad that Tim, one of the elders, had the wisdom to delay telling me of that prophetic word until I had been at Tamworth a couple of years. I think that would have placed undue pressure on a still relatively inexperienced pastor.

Looking back on that prophecy from the juncture of more than a quarter of a century of leading our church, one can now see, at least in part, the fulfilment of his words, though even as I write that sentence I must reiterate that all that has been accomplished has been the Lord's doing. It has been all by his grace — his unmerited, undeserved, unreserved, unconditional, unrestricted, unwarranted, gratuitous love that he has lavished on us. The only part that our church leaders or I played was to think God's thoughts after him, and to be daring enough to be obedient to his voice. It was St. Paul who wrote "by the grace of God I am what I am, and his grace to me was not without effect" (1 Cor. 15:10) when he reflected on how God had taken him, a former persecutor of Christians, to become his apostle to the Gentiles. One gets the distinct

29

impression that he can barely believe that God used someone like him to serve God's purposes. I get that! John Newton knew it too as is evidenced in his wonderful hymn:

> *Amazing Grace, how sweet the sound*
> *That saved a wretch like me;*
> *I once was lost, but now am found,*
> *Was blind but now I see.*

The Tamworth Elim Church is located on a narrow dead-end street with a thriving Anglican church at the other end, acting as spiritual book-ends to its residents. The Anglican church, St. George's, had been led for some time by Charles Beresford, a charismatic vicar with a passion for evangelism. Charles is a likeable, down-to-earth character with a common-touch and was largely responsible for turning the church outward into the community. St. George's flourished under his ministry and added a church hall and church extension to house their growing congregation.

Tamworth Elim Church was the poor relation of St. George's some 150 metres down the bottom of Bamford Street. Being an Anglican church, they had ready-made contacts with the community through hatches, matches and despatches, or christenings, weddings and funerals, if you prefer. Charles, being the outgoing person he is, made the most of every opportunity to reach out to the unchurched community. Whilst I was thrilled to see what God was doing through St. George's, and for which I thanked God, I was a little envious — not sure whether I should admit that — at their success in reaching out to the community in a way that we could only have dreamed. I knew that we would not have the same power of attraction. We didn't do christenings. The only weddings that were performed at Elim were those of existing congregation members. No one would ever opt to get married in what looked like an air-raid shelter. Similarly, funerals always went to the parish church.

The biggest challenge in those early years was how to reach out to the community in new, creative and engaging ways. Excuse my stating the obvious, but unless you are regularly rubbing shoulders with people of no faith, you are not going to reach them with the love of Christ. Pretty basic, eh? We knew that we needed to be innovative, as just preaching the gospel to the already converted wasn't going to make any spiritual difference to our community, but we also recognised that our innovation needed to be crafted by God, not just about having good ideas. Since then, our leaders have often spoken about the difference between good ideas and God ideas. Recognising this distinction is so important, as over the years we have on occasions been tempted by good ideas — maybe some kind of community outreach that would have provided us with a new income stream — but resisted because we didn't feel any sense of peace in our hearts or minds; more about that later.

Speaking now as a seasoned veteran of the "pastoral" trenches — yes, I'm old — I recognise that many young leaders overestimate what can be achieved in one year of ministry, but underestimate what can be achieved in five years of ministry. This is a common failing, maybe not only of young leaders! I've known many leaders who have become rather disillusioned and disheartened because they had not witnessed sufficient change or growth within the span of 12 months. When some leaders accept a church's invitation to become the new pastor, they are often wide-eyed and full of faith, and believe they are God's man or woman in that place, anticipating that God is going to do some pretty startling things, but one year later when nothing much has happened and there is nothing to write home about, or worse still, nothing to talk about in their leaders' fraternal, they become disheartened. If you are a church leader, don't you hate it when your colleagues ask, "How many people do you get on a Sunday?" when your church is static, or is even decreasing in size? Alternatively, how elated you feel when things are going well, the church is growing, the offerings are increasing, and you need to add a new service or building extension. I know that it shouldn't be like that, because we are only instruments in God's work and he is the Lord of the harvest, but in our need for approval, and because of our own insecurities, we often yearn for the endorsement of our colleagues and friends. The success of others can be one of our greatest challenges in ministry. The obvious antidote to those pangs of envy is that we get to a place where we begin to accept ourselves as sons and daughters of God and learn that our identity is found in the Lord alone. Basically, you will never know who you are, until you know Whose you are!

One year is not long enough to gauge what God is doing, or what God has started to do, in your ministry. It is far better to think in terms of five years. If you are a church leader, I'll leave that thought with you.

Having been at the helm of our new charge for six months, I realised that there was a pressing problem. Whilst we were a happy church — some might say a happy-clappy church; the music in Tamworth, although good, was a child of its day, with its repertoire often focusing on the triumphal tunes of Graham Kendrick's *March for Jesus* — we were not attracting anyone to our services. The only new people that came to our church were those disenfranchised from other churches in the town. In those days there were a number of people that I called spiritual gypsies, who viewed themselves as a part of the "Christian community" but were not willing to join an actual church, which wasn't particularly helpful to churches in the town or indeed to their own spiritual welfare. Being the new guy in town meant that this roaming cohort descended on our church, not all at once, but in dribs and drabs, giving the impression of church growth, but not really. Whilst a growing congregation can give our egos a lift, I think it is important that churches experience the right kind of growth. In my heart of hearts, I knew that as quickly as they had arrived they would also leave again when the next new pastor came to town. It was my practice then, as it is now, wherever possible, to speak to the leader of the church from where the new attendee arrived. If it appeared that someone was settling with us, I would also encourage him or her to speak with their former pastor rather than just go missing. This practice helped stem the tide of church-hopping and was reciprocated with some church leaders, though not all, and helped to build trust and friendship between these leaders. These days, as in any town, there remains some movement of people, but nothing to the degree of the early 1990s. Thank God!

Gracious God,

Your grace causes us to giggle with glee and dance with delight! We are immensely privileged to be recipients of your extravagant love.

Help us to share what you have given us and what you have taught us with our friends and communities. Whatever we do, whoever we are with, may grace be the driving force of our actions.

May we always strive to be faithful servants of our almighty God, and during those times when we can't see the fruit of our efforts, give us the strength to persevere and carry on with the right attitude of heart, knowing that your grace is always sufficient!

Amen.

CHAPTER FOUR

Getting Started

*A major problem and the
solution from a rugby club*

I AM AMONG THAT GROUP OF PASTORS WHO BELIEVE THAT the new incumbent to a pastorate should not make any knee-jerk reactions, or take on new projects, or indeed change too much early on in their ministry. Whilst that is generally a wise thing, I somewhat disregarded my own principles during my honeymoon period at Tamworth. To be honest, I grasped a few nettles when the majority still thought that this young pastor knew what he was doing! Soon after arrival at Tamworth I became aware that we only catered for children up to the age of eight in our one and only Sunday service, not because we were apathetic to children's ministry, but because of our lack of space. Apart from the main auditorium, we had one other room that served as both a crèche area and a teaching room for the children. Like many other churches, we needed to make do with the space we had, but I knew that this needed to change. We needed some extra space and we needed to do something quickly as no young family would join us if we were not catering for their children. The other problem was that we were not serving our own families, as children over the age of eight were expected to sit through a service that was designed for an adult congregation. Sadly, during these fallow years, the majority of children belonging to church families didn't survive church. Maybe Julie and I were especially aware of this dilemma as our own children were aged ten, eight and six at the time of coming to Tamworth.

Knowing my concerns, a church member spoke to me about the possibility of purchasing a portacabin, a temporary building designed to be moved. It belonged to a local rugby club and had been previously used for makeshift dressing rooms. The rugby club had since built permanent dressing room facilities, and this old — actually very old and rather dilapidated — building was now excess to requirements and a bit of an eyesore on their site. I made contact with the rugby club and they were willing to sell this 48-feet long, 12-feet wide portacabin for £800. This was very inexpensive, though still a lot of money for our small congregation. We planned on turning this building into five classrooms and have a place to grow our children's ministry from that one room at the back of our church auditorium. The problem was that we needed planning permission from the local authority, which is always a bit of a dilemma. In practice, the portacabin would take away four car spaces from our 22-space church car park, which wasn't really a major problem as our church was very small at the time and many of the congregation walked to church on a Sunday anyway. The locals weren't too enthralled with the idea of this portacabin, though; firstly, as many of them disliked change of any sort in their community; but secondly, because our immediate next-door neighbour was the village post office whose customers had grown used to unofficially using our car park throughout the week. They feared that using our own car park for church use might somehow impinge on their business! I never really got my head around that one!

We went through all the necessary channels of planning application and were confident of success. However, the *Birmingham Mail* ran a short article on the evening before the Planning Committee was due to meet, stating that the Planning officers had recommended that our application was to be refused the following day. This was disturbing, and I remember how our own house group that night prayed that the local councillors would change their minds about this; at the same time, I was in the other room canvassing as many of the members of the Planning Committee I could get a hold of on the phone that evening. As someone once said, "Pray for a good harvest, but keep on hoeing," meaning that prayer and action go side by side, a principle that has become second nature to us over the years. The decision was made and we were given full planning permission to erect our 48-feet portacabin at the top end of our car park, much to the surprise of our critics. That was to be the first of many future encounters with local residents and council officers over planning applications during the next 25 years.

The day came for the portacabin to be placed. It was a Monday, the busiest day of the week for this narrow, dead-end street of two churches, a post office and some fifty houses, because it was when most people received their benefits from the post office. I remember the day well. The low-loader negotiated a very tight nine-point turn into Bamford Street from the main road. A crane was *in situ* to offload the portacabin into its designated space, and the police, out of necessity, needed to close off the road. I think that the politest way of saying this is, the local residents were not well pleased! Worse still, if this monstrous portacabin had been spanking new, then that would have been one thing, but it wasn't. It had been repainted an awful blue colour, the extremities of the building had sagged terribly, it was covered in mildew and moss, and several windows had been smashed. Even I thought it was a monstrosity, but it was also our lifeline to do something new for our church family. That morning, the skies were blue... and so was the air, though without rushing too quickly to the present, many of our greatest critics would eventually become our friends and supporters as we continued on our journey of community transformation through kingdom principles.

Following this mini-victory, I invited a working party from the church to spend a few Saturdays with me to transform this carbuncle of a building into something a little more respectable. An extra door was added, five classrooms were created, the building was painted, electricity was wired in from the main church building, and some second-hand children's furniture was purchased. All we needed now were some Sunday School teachers. That was quite easy really, for by now, most of the congregation were ready to walk on burning coals to reach out to young families, so I enlisted everyone I could to serve in the Sunday School. It was an opt-out arrangement rather than an opt-in. Some people did opt out, which is understandable, but of our small church family some 25 people, not quite half the congregation, opted in. It was a start of moving forward, and we were thrilled to witness slow but steady growth, especially among younger families.

As I ponder on this and later chapters in our church story, I am reminded of one of those great narratives in the Old Testament book of 2 Kings. In chapter 4, we read of a poor widow coming to the prophet Elisha for help. Her husband who had served Elisha was now dead and she had creditors threatening to come along and take her two sons as slaves. Elisha told her to borrow as many jars from her friends and neighbours as she could, and then pour her remaining olive oil into a jar. The oil miraculously kept filling each container to the brim. The oil stopped flowing only when the last jar was full. This is a lovely picture of God blessing the woman's faith, and of God's provision being as large as this woman's faith and her willingness to obey the prophet. This was not presumption on her part, for she obeyed what God had said through his prophet to borrow the jars; a very important detail. Faith and presumption are most certainly not the same thing. Our equivalent of borrowing jars was to provide a space for increasing our children's ministry and to get the church ready to teach them in response to what we believed that God was revealing to us; and as with the empty jars, the Lord starting filling the empty space.

Father God,

Thank you for blessing us with little victories that add together to make life's tapestry so much brighter! We treasure those moments, Lord.

Help us not to miss opportunities that come our way, but instead, to actively seek openings to serve wider and deeper. Those "widow's jars" look different to each of us in our diverse situations. Show us what they are and what you want us to do, Lord. We choose now to gather our "jars" and wait with faith and a measure of excitement for you to fill them.

Amen.

CHAPTER FIVE

What is in Your Hand?

WE WERE EXPERIENCING A SPIRITUAL MOMENTUM AND I believed that we needed to continue to move forward on our journey of faith. I remember one afternoon as I was asking the Lord what his ideas were for our church, I was quite distinctly reminded of the Lord's question to Moses when he was being commissioned to be God's man to go to Pharaoh.

God asked Moses, "What is in your hand?"

Moses replied, "A staff."

The Lord then commanded that Moses throw it on the ground. The rest of the story is quite well known, of how God turned Moses' staff into a snake and then when Moses, at God's command, reached out to grab the snake by the tail, it became a staff again. "This," said the Lord, "is so that they may believe that the Lord, the God of their fathers — the God of Abraham, the God of Isaac and the God of Jacob — has appeared to you" (Ex. 4:5).

In my conversation with God, I had a distinct sense that God was asking me that same question, "What is in your hand?" I didn't have a staff, but we did have a building. Just over a year previously, the thing that made life so difficult in church-planting in South Wales was not having a building, a centre of operations, a place to call home, but now we had a building that was only being used on Sunday mornings, Thursday evenings for a children's club, and for *ad hoc* occasions.

Whilst I didn't receive a dramatic direction from heaven that afternoon, it was most definitely a "God-moment" and I knew that I should think and pray about this question over the coming weeks. I mused over the question of what God had purposed to do amongst us through using the excellent resource of our building. If you are a church leader then I would suggest that this is a good question to ask yourself too: *What is in my hand? What resource has God blessed me with that I*

37

can use to reach my community? Is it a building? Is it someone in my congregation with particular skills or passion to serve in some way? Is it a good reputation in my town or city? Maybe it is a good financial income, or something else.

Can you imagine what Moses must have thought at that moment when God asked him to declare what was in his hand? He might have thought to himself, *what has a shepherd's staff got to do with anything? It's just a staff. A glorified stick! How is this piece of wood going to help me when I get to Pharaoh's court? There isn't anything extraordinary about a staff.* Here's the rub: what is in our hand may be very ordinary, but it becomes useful to the purposes of God when God anoints it. So, let me ask again, what is in your hand? While it was in Moses' hand it remained a wooden staff; it was only as he released it that it became useful to God's plan and purposes. We worship a God who can take something small like a shepherd's staff, or for that matter two fishes and five loaves, to bless the multitudes.

I often find that God doesn't provide us with the whole picture all at once. If it were only that simple! Can you imagine the conversation?

God: What is in your hand?

Us: We have a building, Lord.

God: Good, now that I've got your attention, I want you to do _____ with it.

Us: OK, Lord, as long as we know with clarity what you are asking of us! Just needed to know!

I'm not so sure that God normally works that way, certainly not in my case. I've already admitted I don't always find it that easy to discern God's will, though on the very rare occasion it has happened to me that way. I'll tell you a little later of one quite astonishing story of how God gave me a clear instruction to do something that was quite off-the-wall and the quite extraordinary way that God responded. However, the Lord doesn't usually provide me with the whole plan all at once, but often drops a verse, an idea, a concept into my head and asks me to think and pray it through.

What often happens next is that my initial thought is added to and developed in some, often unexpected, manner. I might read an article in a newspaper or magazine that has added poignancy given my previous "God-moment", or meet someone quite "coincidentally" who brings a measure of wisdom or guidance without even realising that he or she is saying anything significant, or sometimes an unguarded thought comes quite out of the blue, which acts as the next link in the chain in developing the concept that the Lord had given me in seed thought.

Sometimes, there might be three, four or five such links in the chain, each developing and fine-tuning what God has planned on how to move forward. It is important not to rush to conclusions and keep an open and sensitive heart. Over the years, I have often spoken to our church family about "holding things lightly in our hands". In other words, don't be too quick to say, "This is what the Lord says..." or "The Lord is calling us to do _____." I know that such certainty gives people the impression that you are in touch with the Lord and that you are an amazing leader, but what if you've got it wrong? What if, after declaring, "This is the way of the Lord," it turns out to be more about having an overactive thyroid or your having eaten too much cheese late at night, and that burning in your heart was nothing more than indigestion?

I think that there is a happy balance needed here. On the one hand, leaders need to walk humbly before the Lord acknowledging that God gives us guidance and wisdom, but also admitting it isn't always easy to know exactly what his plan looks like. It is something that we need to sit with, pray over and talk through with wise and godly people, sometimes for several months. The balance to this, of course, is that we don't procrastinate through lack of faith or desire.

Let me come back to the story of God asking Moses what was in his hand. My answer to that same question was that we had a building in our hand. But it was several months before I knew what that might mean for the next step on our church journey.

Over the next few months, there were those other links I talked about. One was a "chance" conversation with an old pastor friend, Rowland, from theological college, at a Bible Week. He informed me that he started a day nursery in his church and that there were some significant benefits to having a nursery, especially in that it provided his church with many great contacts in his community. Basically, people were coming through the church doors who previously had nothing to do with his church; some even started coming to church services on a Sunday and became Christians. Another benefit was that nurseries which are well run can make significant financial profits that can be fed into the church to pay for key staff members, or even can bankroll other church and community projects. To be honest, my heart skipped a beat or two when I had this conversation. Could this be the way forward for our church? Was this what we might use our church building for during the week? Was this the next step in God's plan? My mind was racing. To say that this idea had captured my interest would be putting it mildly. I felt an immediate affinity with this model of outreach. Within days, I was thinking about how we could move forward with such a venture in Tamworth, having regular telephone conversations with my old friend, and doing some research about full day nurseries in the Tamworth area. Up until this time, I hadn't heard of any church venturing out to use its building in this way. I was certainly interested in the concept of using a day nursery as an evangelistic opportunity too, as since the day I came to faith in 1977, personal evangelism has been in my heart. And as I look back over my ministry, I have had the privilege of leading more people into a relationship with Jesus through casual face-to-face conversations than I ever have through pulpit ministry. I so thank God for giving me both the passion and the anointing for this. Julie often comments about the poor unsuspecting people who get to sit next to me on an aeroplane journey for three or four hours. That aside, this idea grabbed my attention, but what would our church eldership think? Would they think "good idea" or "God idea"? Well, I was soon to find out at the next leadership meeting.

Dear Lord,

Thank you that you still choose to communicate with us. Forgive us if we don't always recognise your voice straight away and help us to be increasingly aware and attentive to your leading.

We love to look back at those seemingly coincidental or inconsequential moments that we later realise are all part of your much bigger plan. You are so amazing! We are excited that you can transform the ordinary and commonplace into extraordinary and unexpected achievements. We humbly ask that you direct our thoughts so that we don't miss out on God-given opportunities.

Amen.

CHAPTER SIX

Our First Community Project

*One small step of faith,
one giant leap into our future*

THE LEADERSHIP TEAM COMPRISED AN EASY-GOING, FLEX-
ible, pretty switched-on group of individuals who were as excited as I
was over the possibility of venturing out with our first community project
of a day nursery. They asked to meet my friend, Rowland, requesting
that he supply a business plan based on his experience of running a day
nursery. He had recently moved from his former church and was waiting
for news of a new pastorate, so he was more than happy to help us in our
quest. Following a couple of meetings with him, our church leaders
became convinced that this was a door that God was opening and that
we would be disobedient not to walk through it.

Over the next couple of months, we presented our business plan to
the Elim Church HQ, or "PO BOX 38", as it was affectionately known
in those days, which was its postal address in Cheltenham. Tamworth
Elim Church is a member of the Elim Pentecostal Church, that has 550
churches in the UK and Ireland and is linked to over 4,000 churches
worldwide. As a member church, Tamworth Elim is required to present
its business plans to its head office in Cheltenham (since moved to
Malvern), UK, for approval. The HQ management team approved of our
ideas and were, I think, comforted that we were not reinventing the
wheel, as there was already a tried and tested template for this kind of
community project. They agreed to our vision and granted us a £12,000
bank overdraft to complete some minor alterations to our church
building in order to bring it up to the required standards of the statutory
authority, and to enable us to pay the salaries of our first staff members
for the first couple of months. Our business plan was realistic and

anticipated that we would not make a profit in the first few months. We needed to employ a few staff members in anticipation of receiving children, and the expenditure would be significantly higher than the income at the start, but when more children were signed up, we anticipated moving into a profit.

Since Rowland and his wife, Annette, had gained significant expertise, they were invited to join the ministry team at Tamworth Elim. They were happy to accept joint roles in leading the day nursery, with Rowland also becoming the assistant pastor. They were delighted to join us and I was delighted to be able to extend the pastoral team.

The church building was adapted, Rowland and Annette were employed, and the new nursery was advertised widely. We opened for business on 9th May 1994. The excitement was tangible! There were five staff members, including Rowland and Annette, and one child. However, at the commencement of the nursery, having five staff and one child was difficult. Admittedly, the lad was spoiled rotten, but we had not anticipated how difficult it was to attract new children to a nursery without a track record and without other children being present. Prospective parents would visit and could only see what the day nursery was, rather than what it could be in a couple of months. It lacked atmosphere, understandably. The staff members were also given long, dark blue matron's uniforms to wear, which didn't help with selling the nursery to parents. They were wonderfully friendly people, but they looked like nursing staff from a post-war sanatorium, rather austere and clinical, and to be truthful lost in a bit of a time warp! In time, we changed the uniform to something a bit more colourful and comfortable and not so sterile. How easy it is to look back on our mistakes and have 20:20 vision!

Our new nursery leaders were to report to the church leaders each month. There was no desire to micromanage for, after all, they were the experts, but the church leaders naturally needed to provide financial oversight to this project. A few weeks into the project, Rowland was admitted to a private hospital in Birmingham. He told me that he hadn't been sleeping well and was exhausted, and that he would soon be back at the helm of the day nursery. This was supposedly something that he had experienced previously and would soon be rectified. However, the hospital stay lasted longer than expected and he missed the first month's financial meeting with the church leaders. After the nursery had been running about six weeks it grew to three or four children, which was a vast improvement on having just one child. Poor kid! But I remained concerned that child numbers hadn't grown quickly enough and we were nearly at the limit of our £12,000 overdraft. We were sinking. This was confirmed when the bank statement came through. To make matters worse — *much* worse — I discovered that my friend Rowland was suffering some kind of nervous breakdown of which sleep deprivation was a symptom. His condition was more serious than just being deprived of sleep. Several years later I discovered the probable cause for his illness was that he had been shot and injured whilst serving as a paratrooper in Northern Ireland and had been haunted by his memories of his time there, and had suffered from post-traumatic stress disorder for many years.[5]

The day nursery had been running six weeks and we were on the precipice of going out of business. This was incredibly scary on many fronts. We had previously shared our plans with the church congregation claiming that this was in fact God's vision for the church. We had communicated all the benefits, such as the chance to meet with young families in our community, the opportunities for evangelism, the prospect of employing other staff members on our church ministry team, and also the opportunity to financially support other future church ministries. Our church family believed that we had heard from God and when they had witnessed the commencement of our day nursery, faith was running high. But if this "vision" was to come to an abrupt end in less than two months, it could have a disastrous effect on people's faith and also on their confidence in the church leaders, especially this new, rather in-experienced young pastor from South Wales. They would not be so quick to embrace any future vision. Once bitten, twice shy, as they say.

Most of the church family, but not all, had initially bought into this vision of a day nursery. I say "not all" as some people actually left the church claiming that by starting a day nursery we were "pandering to the middle classes" in providing a service for only those who could afford it, and neglecting the poorest, and that we should not be entertaining such an idea as it wasn't God's will. These were the days before government-subsidised nursery places. Whilst we knew this allegation was untrue as

---

[5] *Telegraph and Argus*, 24th December 2011, article by Hannah Baker, 'Care Home for veterans tells ill Wyke man they can't look after him', *www.thetelegraphandargus.co.uk/news/localbrad/9438064.Care_home_for_veterans_tells_ill_Wyke_man_they_can___t_look_after_him*

our desire was to reach all people from all strata of society and backgrounds, and that any financial profit would be used towards helping the vulnerable and needy in society, it might have appeared to some that those who "jumped ship" were right all along — it wasn't God's will!

An emergency church leadership meeting was held and conversations were had with our denomination's HQ who had previously agreed to our having an overdraft facility to get us up and running. These conversations on how to rescue this fledgling community project were challenging in the extreme, and the conclusion was pretty unpalatable. To cut a long story — and many sleepless nights — short, our head office agreed that we could increase our overdraft facility to £18,000 which would give us the opportunity to turn around the day nursery. But that was as far as they were willing to go: £18,000 and no more, but on the proviso that we lost a couple of staff members! This is where it got really difficult as the only staff we could lose were those who were supernumerary, namely our friends who had come to Tamworth to establish the nursery. Another factor was that they were on a considerably higher salary than rank-and-file nursery nurses. This decision was made so much harder as Rowland was suffering with a mental health problem at the time. It was as simple as that, but it didn't make the conversations any easier. Leadership is not for wimps as hard decisions need to be made which are sometimes terribly painful!

Even now, a quarter of a century on, I get sweaty palms at the thought of those awkward, and what must have seemed like hurtful, conversations. There was only one feasible option, and it needed to be done. Our friends left and we were all bruised by this painful episode, though to this day I cannot think of another option that was open to us. Rowland has since passed away, and I am sorry that I didn't ever get an opportunity to catch up with him again at some later date, but I look forward to that day when I shall meet him again and we can embrace.

We were left with the job of turning around this fledgling day nursery. We needed to keep a tight ship financially; we advertised widely, held open days, and a couple of months later the leaders asked Julie, who is a qualified primary school teacher, to head up the nursery on a part-time basis, which she did for a period of 14 months, just long enough to help us through the critical time. Our hard work paid off, though each month we could see the overdraft rising, and it reached its highest point of £17,994 in December 1994. We remained conscious of the plug being pulled at £18,000, though in retrospect I doubt that with a far better business projection our HQ would have been so fastidious or short-sighted as to close us down. Our nursery made a profit for the first time in January 1995, and has since been a significant creator of wealth for our church and the later Manna House charity, with all of its profits being fed back into central funds in order to serve the purposes of God through a range of community projects. Looking back, I can now see how critical the success of our day nursery has been to everything that we have sought to do in serving God in Tamworth.

One of our original junior staff members, June Emmerson, whose husband Paul served as a church elder and later associate pastor, has been the cornerstone of our nursery since the day the doors opened. June, for many years now, has served as Head of Nursery, and 25 years on is still doing a wonderful job!

Lord,

Thank you for the excitement of new opportunities and also for wonderful people who diligently work in projects long after they are not new anymore and when the day-to-day routines don't seem quite so exciting! Help us all to persevere when life gets complicated and things don't go to plan.

We especially ask for your grace when we have to make tough decisions that cause upset and pain to people we care deeply about, or when the decisions of others cause us to suffer. May we never be blasé in those circumstances, Lord, and help us to turn to you for wisdom, strength and healing at all times and on all occasions.

Amen.

CHAPTER SEVEN

Expanding the Team

WITHIN THE FIRST YEAR OF OUR DAY NURSERY IT WAS OUR joy to employ Clive and Michele. When I served in the City Church in Cardiff, Clive was just a young guy of about 18 who had a spiritual maturity beyond his age. He was also an accomplished worship leader. He was his own person and a guy of great integrity, and had a wonderful sense of humour. I was aware that Clive had left Cardiff, got married and worked for a Christian conference centre in Torquay as a chef. I knew that he would be someone I could work with and would bring something quite special to our team at Tamworth. Basically, I was looking for a part-time chef and a part-time administrator for the increasing paperwork of our growing nursery. I believed those could be tent-making roles for Clive and Michele much in the way that the Apostle Paul funded his own apostolic ministry whilst dedicating himself to the work of sharing the Good News of Jesus.[6]

I had no way of contacting Clive, but got his phone number through a mutual friend, Mike Sherwood, who had been the senior pastor of our church in Cardiff. In one of those wonderful God-incidences, Mike told me that he had not seen Clive for a very long time but that Clive had recently sought him out for advice on taking a next step forward in serving the Lord. Could this be a coincidence? I thought not. I rang Clive and invited him and Michele to come to Tamworth to chat through the prospect of him being a part-time nursery chef in the mornings, and the rest of the time serving as a youth pastor. Michele, who had excellent administration skills, could work part-time for the nursery and part-time for the church, with the day nursery footing the bill for both salaries. We were still a very small church of about 70 people on a good day. The only

---

[6] See Acts 18:3 where Paul supported his ministry in Corinth through tent-making.

catch was, we didn't have any young people! But again, our thinking was quite intentional: we would get a youth pastor before we got the youth. Clive would have afternoons to reach out to young people through schools work and would be in place to get alongside church children who were getting to secondary school age. We believed that it was important to get the structure and personnel in place to capture what we believed God was going to do amongst us. Remember again that story of Elisha and the widow who was asked to collect empty jars?

Clive and Michele spent four years in Tamworth before moving to pastures new. They were wonderful years, full of faith and fun. Sadly, however, Clive contracted non-Hodgkin's lymphoma, a cancer that starts in white blood cells, which are part of the body's immune system. This was a desperate time for them, a time during which Clive wrote and produced two excellent musical albums. The first was entitled *Teach Me To Trust* after the title song, which is occasionally still sung at our church some 20-something years on:

Your thoughts are so much higher than mine,
I see so dimly at times,
Your ways are so much higher than mine,
And yet You care about my life.
Teach me to trust You,
Teach me to hold to You,
Teach me to walk with You,
Even though sometimes I'm blind.
Teach me to run to You,
Teach me to come to You,
Teach me to trust You, Lord,
And Your plan for my life.

Those words remain deeply embedded in our church DNA and they continue to speak to me with such power and poignancy. Music has always had a major role to play in the life and worship of Tamworth Elim, and today we are blessed beyond measure with our excellent worship team led by Bob, Tim and Simon, each bringing their distinctive styles to this ministry.

Clive and Michele had one child, but feared that due to Clive's cancer treatment regime no further children would be possible. They were wrong. Clive got through the treatment and the Sunday morning came that he announced to the church that Michele was expecting again, with cheers and applause and wolf-whistles coming from the congregation. Clive, who was a master of accents, in his best "broad Yorkshire" said, "Nowt rong wi' uz plumbing!" which left everyone in fits of laughter. Only he could get away with it!

Father God,

Thank you for the positive impact made by those who are willing to work in just about any capacity in order to serve you; for those whose faith and joy run deep, sometimes in spite of their circumstances, and whose presence brings something of the lightness of your Spirit into the most ordinary of gatherings!

Faith and joy like this come through knowing that even though your thoughts and ways are so much higher than ours, you don't distance yourself from us, but draw close and promise to be with us, whatever our situation. Teach us to trust you, Lord!

Amen.

CHAPTER EIGHT

More than a Building Project

A real game-changer!

IT WAS HARD TO BELIEVE THAT WE HAD BEEN AT TAM-
worth less than three years when another opportunity opened up before
us. As I've said previously, I had no intention of making too many early
changes, but it appears that the Lord had other things in mind. In 1995,
I became aware that our county council might be selling ground adjacent
to the church, on the main Glascote Road leading to the town centre.

In 1969, the Elim Church had moved from its old corrugated tin
church building the other side of town to a new home in Bamford Street,
Glascote. The Elim Church purchased a building that had previously
belonged to the Primitive Methodists. The congregation worshipped
there for eight years until 1977 when the council took out Compulsory
Purchase Orders on the old church and other properties on Glascote
Road, with the intention of widening the main road into the town centre.
The old church was knocked down and a new one (i.e. the "air-raid
shelter") immediately adjacent was built in its place.

The council's intention was to widen the main road, but it never
happened! The result was that the other, now empty buildings purchased
by the council became more dilapidated and run-down as the years
progressed. To be truthful, the five properties with their two adjoining
car parks which were adjacent to the new Elim Church became an eyesore and an embarrassment to the village of Glascote. Windows were
smashed, wooden doors were full of graffiti, brickwork displayed
crumbling mortar from when the houses were built over one hundred
years previously, and the properties were also used as places for drug
parties. Apart from that, no problem!

On the back of the success of the portacabin and then the
commencement of the day nursery, I believed that God was presenting us

49

with a once-in-a-lifetime opportunity. Can you imagine? Five derelict properties and two car parks — this was our opportunity to serve God in the new and creative ways that we so yearned. If we could only get our hands on this site, it could be used to reimagine church. So, I made contact with the county council and spoke about the possibility of purchasing the entire site of five terraced houses and enough room for an extra 28 car spaces in a highly populated area — sheer gold dust in a built-up residential zone!

Remember I mentioned the story of Elisha and the widow who needed to go to her neighbours to get as many empty jars as they could lend her? Same principle again! We were confident that God was in the middle of this "coincidence" and was going to bless us, but we also needed to build our vision on solid business plans. We couldn't just go off on some tangent or some half-baked idea with the expectation that God would bless poor preparation. Indeed, there are times that God works in spite of us, but we shouldn't ever assume that he will bless poor preparation or shoddy workmanship or unsound business planning.

This was considerably bigger than just getting an £18,000 bank overdraft as for our day nursery. This was a project that would be in the hundreds of thousands of pounds. I hadn't any training in these sorts of things. I had no education to write home about, other than a couple of very poor A-levels, no experience of buildings, project management, planning applications, tendering, grant applications, commissioning work, and the like. If they ever taught this at theological college, I must have been off sick that day. We are talking of stuff that was well out of my comfort zone, and probably yours too, but we need to remember that God uses the weak and foolish things (people) of this world. I certainly fitted into that category!

I found that this was a matter of spinning plates. At the time I was speaking to the county council about the possibility of purchasing these awful, wonderful properties, I needed to simultaneously perform other tasks, such as:

- *Speaking to our church HQ and through them to our bank about how we could fund this project.* This vision needed to be founded on solid business principles and a robust financial basis, as one can have all the vision in the world but such projects need to be paid for!

- *Engaging in dreaming dreams with our leaders of what we might use these properties for to serve the purposes of God.* We were open to just about anything as long as God was in it. Our motivation was to honour him and extend his kingdom.
- *Speaking with local councillors to ascertain what the greatest needs were that we might help support.* For example, I thought that some of the derelict properties might be used for housing the homeless, though that wasn't given the same priority by the council. Their greatest need was to house adults with severe learning disabilities within the community rather than their being placed in an institution.
- *Applying for external funding from trust funds as we didn't possess any significant capital.* Some charitable organisations these days often have fund managers who are expert in writing applications to grant-giving charities, but all we had was a three-volume directory of grant-giving charitable trusts that exist to give good causes financial help... and me! All this was also before the days of doing a Google search! Do you remember how we lived our lives before emails, Google and instant access to a world of knowledge? It's hard to believe that our lives have changed so much in only a couple of decades.
- *Applying for outline planning consent.* This was very important as we could have done everything else but still failed if we did not get planning permission approved.

When I was ministering in Cardiff some years before, Julie and I quite often visited a great combined Christian bookshop and coffee shop in a suburb north of the city. The Olive Branch was a community outreach of a local Baptist church, and was a warm, welcoming, attractive place to meet friends, as well as a great resource to many Christians in the city. I believed that at least part of our development was to be used as a bookshop and coffee shop following The Olive Branch model, though in later years we discovered that this model needed to be adapted and changed quite considerably. Unlike the suburb of Cardiff, which was quite middle-class with a fair share of professional people, Tamworth is essentially white working-class, and our village isn't a particularly well-to-do area, with few having disposable income. I'll tell you more about these changes later, but suffice to say at this point that God doesn't always provide us with the full picture all at once.

In addition to having our own bookshop and coffee shop, we planned on using the site to service our own church ministries, including our children's work which was growing beyond the space available in the portacabin. The properties would also be used to house our growing youth group and offices. It was our desire to reach out to some vulnerable or disenfranchised groups of people, but we weren't sure at this stage what particular social need we would serve. We were open to offers!

Once the leaders were convinced that we should move forwards with this vision of purchasing a row of derelict properties adjacent to our church site, we needed to speak to a specially convened meeting of our church family. I say *family* rather than *membership* for two reasons. Firstly, the metaphor of family built on love, trust and good relationships more accurately describes our people than a membership, which sometimes has the connotation of subscribing to a club through the payment of fees in order to receive the benefit of being a member of that club. Family is much more personal. The second reason why I don't speak of church membership is because we don't have one in any formal sense. Those who are part of the church family know that they belong. They don't need to sign a piece of paper to prove it. I can already hear some church leaders wince loudly at that concept and are penning at least half a dozen reasons why membership is better. All I want to say is, this model works really well for us.

So, we called a special meeting of our church family. The previous occasion we called such a gathering was when the leaders presented the concept of hosting a day nursery in our church building, a vision that eventually came good and was a blessing to the church. Some nursery parents and staff members were added to the church through the nursery outreach. So, when a special meeting was called to talk through the next stage in our church vision, just about everyone who classed Tamworth Elim as their spiritual home attended, perhaps out of intrigue as much as anything else. What could be next?

Following a time of worship, I addressed the congregation. I informed them that this was a once-in-a-lifetime opportunity. If we were to ignore this opportunity, then it simply wouldn't ever be presented to us again. I declared that this was important — *really* important — a strategic moment in our church's history. As you can see, I didn't mince my words. As ever, you will have the early "adopters" which included all the leaders who were on board. Others were cautious but open to this being the right way forward. Then there were a few people, with frowned brows and icy stares, who looked very concerned indeed. There was a mixed response, though generally positive as we had won a certain amount of credit for the way that we had rescued the nursery project. However, towards the end of the discussion time, one gentleman stated, "You are going to bleed us dry!" referring to the obvious costs which were going to be well in excess of a quarter of a million pounds. "Where is this money coming from?" he added. "We are only a small church with limited finances!"

Before I tell you how I answered this guy, I want to say, as is often said on certain reality TV shows, "Don't try this at home!" — good advice to viewers who might attempt some apparently unwise action. What I am going to say is *not* something I recommend, but I record it simply because it is what I actually said on the night. Now that we are clear about that, in response to this guy's rather negative words, I said that it was my intention not to ask the church family for a single penny towards this project. How could anyone refuse an offer like that? To tell you the truth, although my leadership team was confident that this opportunity was from God, I'm not so sure that they agreed with my apparent gung-ho response, though no one challenged me on it. Even though I do not recommend my course of action to any young pastor reading this, I was so confident that God was in this project that out of the fullness of my heart my mouth spoke! Without rushing too far ahead, I kept my promise and did not ask our small church congregation for a single penny.

Whilst I do not wish to labour the point and bore my readers to sleep with the minutiae of a building project, I do want to say a little bit more about this, and for a couple of reasons. Firstly, I would not want anyone to think that being a leader is only about dreaming dreams, vision casting and acts of triumphant faith. It does include those elements, but equally it is about perseverance, hard work, common sense and talking to others who are more gifted in areas of finance and technical aspects of building projects. Basically, I want to disavow readers of the idea that extending God's kingdom through great building schemes is a glorious and pain-free adventure of faith.

Secondly, I want to provide any church leaders, pastors, priests, elders, deacons or those involved in some capacity of church leadership, with some idea of what might be involved in such building projects. This isn't for the squeamish, but if God is truly in your project then go for it with passion, dare to trust him, and may God be honoured! So, if you are not a church leader who is pondering a building project, the next few paragraphs might not be the most edifying thing you've read in your life. Even so, I hope that you stay with me, because I think it is a great story and to purchase these redundant buildings was critical to our future ministry. Actually, I'd go as far as to say that this was probably the key moment in our church's history. That is some statement, I know! Putting it negatively, without these buildings Tamworth Elim Church would be reduced to being a small church in a dead-end road, suffocated by terraced houses and sole traders.

OK, let's be practical now!

In the early days of dreaming dreams, I met up with a local Labour councillor who sat on both borough and county councils. He was very helpful in finding out what were the greatest priorities in the community of Glascote, our immediate patch. If anyone should know, it would be the council. It is so important to do your homework and not merely assume that you have the right plan through anecdotal evidence or a warm fuzzy feeling. I was guilty of this myself. I thought that our community's greatest need was to build housing for the homeless, but the council, for good reasons, thought otherwise. They redirected us to housing adults with special educational needs. For us, this was really important because to help meet the council's objectives would also mean that we could potentially receive funding from them. There were other similar projects running in the county and there was an existing template for this kind of project, so all we needed to do was name our price. Tricky! Actually, very tricky! Especially for someone who was a rank amateur with no idea where to gauge an appropriate figure. Would they laugh out loud at my cheek at quoting a figure simply off the scale, or alternatively, be amused by us asking for nowhere near enough? Thankfully, one of the county council's commissioners accidentally "let slip" with the figures from another project — which sounded pretty good to me!

The county council requested that we supply housing for three adults with special needs and they would provide a 24-hour care package. Of the five derelict houses, we planned on using one-and-a-half for this scheme and the other three-and-a-half for all the other church and charity work. This, as most of the things I've ever been involved in, was well out of my comfort zone as I needed to negotiate legal contracts with the council. The need to read all the small print, over 40 pages in all, understand it, make comment and on occasions disagree with it, was excruciating for a very ordinary young pastor who had no legal training, but it was necessary. This wasn't brilliant bedtime reading, but neither is reading Leviticus! Did I just say that?

Having worked out the figures, I reasoned that if we could get the council to formally agree to our price, we would not only be able to provide housing for adults with special educational needs, which we really had a heart to do, but also receive enough revenue to service the mortgage on the whole project. Yes, you heard me correctly! All five houses and two car parks! There was a slight problem, however. Our bank manager said he could not support this project as we needed £70,000 as a down-payment. But where were we to get this money? This was a big ask for us!

I had committed myself to not asking for a "single penny" from our church, but knowing our plight, Les and Karin, a couple from our church, offered a loan of £35,000. Les owned his own building company; and they were as big-hearted, generous and magnanimous a couple as you would ever meet. Les was renowned for his barbeques. His chopping best cuts of steak and throwing them on to the charcoal fire was memorable, though he was also renowned for having a few drinks too many at these events. Les was a wonderful character and a lovely, godly friend who passed away in 2013 — a bloke's bloke whom I miss so much. We agreed to pay back Les and Karin's loan after five years and needed to include these payments in our business plan. In addition to this loan, the county council offered to provide a further loan of £30,000. Not just a loan, but an interest free loan which was only to be paid back at the end of the 15-year contract with them. Astonishing! It was one thing saving up to pay back Les and Karin, but how were we to pay back £30,000? The answer to that question, and you'll love this, was that the church leaders took out an endowment policy on my life. Each month a regular amount was paid into this policy and it was expected to mature with sufficient money to pay back the loan after 15 years. That worked out well. As you can see, we really were amateurs at this stuff. There was one further significant amount to come our way, though this time it was a gift rather than a loan.

I had applied to the Tudor Trust, a large trust fund in central London. Their senior executive came to visit the site. He appeared to be impressed with what he heard about community transformation from this young pastor, but I couldn't really tell if he would support our bid or not. I remember him asking me how much we wanted. What a question! I was very aware that I could get this quite wrong by asking for too much or too little. To tell you the truth, I would have been happy with anything they were willing to give us.

I took a deep breath and without blinking I answered with the words, "£70,000." There, I said it. There was no turning back now.

The senior executive didn't flinch, splutter, smirk, snort or laugh out loud. He just said, "OK!"

We waited some weeks and were told of the day that the decision was to be made.

The day of reckoning came. I was like a cat on a hot tin roof. At lunchtime I needed to leave my office and work from home for a few hours, but left a message with our then head of nursery, Sandra, to make contact with me as soon as the promised fax was sent through. These were the days before texts or even emails. About 3:30pm, she rang me at home.

"The fax is coming through now," she said.

"What does it say? What does it say? Have they awarded us any grant?" I responded.

"I don't know. It's a few pages long and the details are still coming through," she said.

They had approved our application and awarded £35,000, half of what we requested, but an amazing gift nevertheless. They took a chance on us and I am forever grateful to the Tudor Trust who helped get us moving into our community ventures (better "adventures"). Trust funds like to do business with organisations, churches and charities that have a good track record. That would have, and should have, counted us out, for we had only set up a community day nursery the previous year. We didn't have anything going for us other than a dream and trust in our God that this project was really from him and that we were stepping out in obedience to his purposes.

The bank agreed to our business plans. We purchased the entire site by closed tender, which was another trial as we were competing against other potential buyers. Some wanted only part of the site for their personal use. I remember a local dentist wanting to do a deal with us, in that she would have one house that could be converted into a dental practice and we could have the rest of the site, but we knew that for our plan to work we needed all five houses and two car parks. Fearing that we would be outbid by our competitors, we placed a bid in for £80,000, which doesn't seem much now for such a large plot of ground, but it was as much as we could afford as we were on a shoestring budget. Coming a close second in the tendering wasn't an option. There could be only one winner and — praise God! — it was us.

We won the tender, and the building contract was won by Les, which so pleased me, especially since he and Karin had been prepared to take a massive risk on this project with their personal finances. You all know that faith is often spelled R-I-S-K, right? This was far more than just another job to Les; he was chomping at the bit to get started, but needed to wait until the conveyancing was processed and contracts signed. In fact, knowing that the proposed day for completion of contracts was one Monday in April 1996, in anticipation he had arranged his workforce to be ready to move speedily the following day. That morning I took our kids to school by 8:45am and needed to drive by the site. I was astonished to witness about 20 guys there, with diggers clearing the ground and with lorries disposing of the rubbish. They had already been working for a couple of hours. My heart leapt for joy to see God so evidently at work!

The home for three adults with special educational needs was completed for them to move into by early August 1996. Whilst the residents of the house, known locally as Glascote House, changed over the years, Anne remained, not only as a house resident, but as a committed follower of Jesus belonging to our church. Being a part of a loving, caring church family has changed her life. The special needs house relocated one mile up the road in 2013, but Anne and Caroline, two of the three residents, continue to attend Elim Church. These days we have also added a monthly celebration service that is aimed at those with special educational needs, their families and friends. It is called Lighthouse, and as its name suggests, Lighthouse is a gathering that shines the light of Christ to those with learning difficulties, championed expertly by Linda and her team. Anne and Caroline, and more recently others, have become such a loved and important part of a church community that values and accepts them just as they are — a church that celebrates diversity and seeks to integrate people of all abilities, and from all walks of life, into its mission. Anne regularly and conscientiously folds paper napkins for our Coffee Shop ministry every Friday afternoon — an important ministry, for Anne and for us! Caroline has no inhibition and likes to dance in our services, but hey, there's nothing wrong with that. She exhibits a freedom that comes from being valued by her extended family.

The second phase of The Manna House, aptly named as we believe that these game-changing buildings were as much a gift of God's grace and faithfulness as was the manna provided daily to the nation of Israel in the Sinai Desert, was completed in early October 1996. I remember the excitement at the handover of the completed buildings from Les's building company so well. It was a Friday afternoon, and I walked from my home to the site and was quite overwhelmed by Les's "finishing touch" to months of building works. Without my knowing, he erected a large wooden cross, which had been polished and rubbed down many times, with the words "To God be all the glory!" engraved. That was Les's prayer, and it was mine too, that God would receive all the glory and that his Name would be praised and honoured through this new centre.

Dear Lord,

Thank you for always being with us and for turning negatives into positives and obstacles into opportunities.

We are especially grateful that you are with us when we are far away from our comfort zones! It is often in those times that our faith is increased and we learn more about you and your ways than at any other time.

We thank you, too, for placing in our path people from whom we can seek wise counsel. Guard us from becoming too arrogant to seek advice, Lord, and let us grow in wisdom as we navigate life's opportunities and upheavals.

Amen.

Our Lighthouse group members are never camera shy!

CHAPTER NINE

Making Maximum Impact

THE MANNA HOUSE COFFEE SHOP, WHERE YOU COULD GET a great three-course meal for £5, became a favourite watering hole for many local people. This ministry was headed up by Paul Emmerson, one of our church elders, who gave up a good job in sales management to take a much lower paid position as Centre Manager. Paul was one of those people who are great to have around, a solid and dependable guy who often picked up those jobs that wouldn't otherwise get done. Paul gave this fledgling ministry solidity from day one. He served in this capacity for seven years before taking on the role as associate pastor at our church, serving for another eight years in a range of ministry tasks, including work with the elderly and in prison ministry. Paul eventually got ordained as an Elim minister and accepted a pastorate in an inner-city Birmingham Elim church before becoming a full-time prison chaplain. All I can say is that the development of our church's community ministry would have been much more difficult without someone as reliable as Paul, whose ministry complemented my own for fifteen or so years.

Four years since my induction as pastor in 1992 had passed; we were now slowly but surely moving forward in mission and were becoming the church that God was calling us to be. To call our model of church at that time "incarnational" would actually be anachronistic. "Incarnational" is a term used in church circles for churches like ours some years later. For those who are completely lost over what I've just written, the incarnation speaks of God becoming human in the birth of Christ. Essentially, God comes to where we are, sits where we sit, and stands where we stand, so an incarnational church is one that brings Christ to its community by coming alongside its community in a Christ-like manner. That is what we have sought to do for the last quarter of a century. Amy Carmichael once said, "It may be that decisions which seem to change the character of the work will have to be made. But if the root principles which have governed us from the beginning are held fast, there will be no real change. The river may flow in a new channel, but it will be the same river."[7] Over the years, there have been many new channels for outreach, to young and old and everyone in between, but it is the same river that we are rowing in, the river of community outreach through meeting the needs of our community in very practical ways, winning the right to proclaim the Good News of Jesus, the one who has changed our lives and who motivates us to serve his purposes in the manner we do.

Early on in my ministry I came across a simple formula from an excellent book by Bill Hybels and Mark Mittelberg, *Becoming a Contagious Christian.*[8]

High Potency	+	Close Proximity	+	Clear Communication	=	Maximum Impact

The impact for God and his kingdom that our small church has made is largely down to this rationale. It would appear that for some time before Julie and I arrived in Tamworth, the church had lost its ability, possibly its confidence, in reaching out to those outside its walls. Very few people without a church background ever came through its doors, and to say there was a "disconnect" with its community would be putting it mildly. We were singing the great tunes of marching in the victory of God, but that's all we were doing — singing!

I proposed to the church leaders of the time that we needed to live our lives in *close proximity* to people who do not think like us, people who don't have Christian friends or families, or even a Bible in their homes. We needed to look for as many ways as we could to sit where they sit, and to reach across the divide to meet them either in their world or on neutral ground. As has often been said, we (Christians) will be the only Bible that many people will ever have a chance to "read". In Tamworth, we had made a start in this regard. Our day nursery was staffed by both Christians and those with no faith or church affiliation. Parents who used our services were both from the church family and from

---

[7] Griffiths, Stephen, *The Axe and the Tree,* Oxford, Lion Hudson, 2017, 67.

[8] Hybels, B., and Mittelberg, M., *Becoming a Contagious Christian,* Grand Rapids, Zondervan, 1994, 50-65.

the wider community. This presented us with great opportunities to speak of the love of God to people not associated with our church.

Then, just a couple of years later, we had the opportunity to reach out and reimagine church in new and creative ways by hosting a coffee shop that was open to the whole community. It was so wonderful to rub shoulders on a daily basis with people we would not have otherwise met had it not been through the means of the coffee shop. It was never intended to make money. In fact, we hoped that one day we might get close to breaking even, but that wasn't the point. It was there to provide people with "spiritual" as well as "physical" nourishment. All the staff were believers and often got the opportunity to share their faith, especially with our regulars, in an easy-going and friendly manner. Many churches will have a budget for evangelism, and use it in hosting special events, or purchasing good evangelistic literature, or hiring an evangelist. We chose to spend our limited budget in supporting a coffee shop ministry. Each year, for a number of years, the coffee shop made a financial loss, but the big question for us concerned the amount of financial loss that we could justify in the name of evangelism. That became a heart-searching question for us some years later, especially in 2009 when the country was experiencing an economic downturn.

The Christian bookshop was largely used by Christians — no surprises there — but not entirely. The service was also of benefit to local schools looking for good Christian materials for school projects and classroom teaching. Many came to our bookshop for gifts, often Bibles, for the various rites of passage — christenings, weddings and funerals. We didn't get much call for circumcisions and bar mitzvahs! Seriously, only eternity will tell of the impact of many of these wonderful conversations. Each one was helping to break down another barrier. This again was a child of its day and might not be as effective in our Internet age where resources can be so easily purchased via Amazon and be delivered the following day.

Close proximity with unbelievers is essential — we will not see people coming to trust Jesus if we don't get alongside them — but that on its own isn't enough. Some Christians have regular contact with those who are not Christians, but instead of drawing them closer to Jesus, sadly, they push them further away. Why is that? Well, firstly, I believe that some of my fellow believers, although sincere and genuine, actually get in the way of their own message through their God-talk which is full of religious clichés, platitudes and banalities that mean very little to your average Joe or Mary Bloggs. There have been times when I have observed well-meaning and sincere Christians share their faith in Christ with poor, unsuspecting unchurched people, and I have not known where to put myself out of sheer embarrassment. My guess is that many of you know exactly what I am talking about! When you think of it, even the word "saved", so often used in a Christian context, is actually quite meaning-less unless carefully unpacked and explained for today's world. The same too when Christians talk about being "born again" or being "redeemed", "bought with a price" and so forth. If we assume that people know nothing, and for the large majority that is the case, then we might get somewhere. We, in the UK at least, are living in a post-Christian culture.

Even if it is conceded that Britain was once a Christian nation — not that I am even slightly convinced by this — it most certainly isn't now. It is probably better to speak of it as once "Christianised". Secondly, I believe that some people are turned away from the Christian faith because some Christians' lives do not match up to their profession of faith. That is what Bill Hybels is focusing on when he makes reference to *"high potency"*. Basically, Christians need to walk their talk (I so want to say that with a Texan drawl!) High potency Christians don't get in the way of their own message!

Close proximity, or choosing to regularly rub shoulders with un-believers, also requires Christians to live authentic and genuine lives, lives that are attractive and appealing, shining Christ's light even when they are not mentioning his name. When one views some soap operas, one is often confronted by a Christian who is caricatured as a grumbling, small-minded, argumentative... yet Bible-quoting hypocrite — basically, some-one you wouldn't want to live next door to, on earth or in heaven! Not a pleasant or attractive sight. However, if a Christian is truly living out the life of Christ (high potency), displaying the fruit of the Spirit of love, joy, peace, patience, kindness, goodness, faithfulness, gentleness and self-control (Gal. 5:2-23), such a high potency life will leave its mark on others. Of course, these qualities aren't the preserve of Christians only, but if we live out these values of a self-giving life of preferring the needs of others, placing their interests before their own, acting justly, loving mercy and walking humbly (see Mic. 6:8), then such a radical counter-cultural example will be hugely appealing. Without the need to "Bible-bash" some poor, unsuspecting person into submission, such an authentic life will maybe cause the other person to ask the reason for the hope that we have. Peter encourages us to "...always be prepared to give an answer to everyone who asks you to give the reason for the hope that you have" (1 Pet. 3:15), and when they ask, we need to make sure that our answer to that question is wise and Christ-like.

When a church starts moving forward in faith, not everyone is pleased. This is something that we find in the combined narrative of Ezra and Nehemiah. When the Jews returned from the Babylonian exile under Zerubbabel to rebuild their Temple, and some years later when they were rebuilding the walls of the city under Nehemiah, there was significant opposition. This is par for the course. Paul writes to the church at Corinth that he was intending to stay on at Ephesus until Pentecost "…because a great door for effective work has opened to me, and there are many who oppose me" (1 Cor. 16:9). When we reclaimed our church car park and placed a portacabin there to house our children's work, not everyone was pleased. One lady, especially, was not pleased — Doris. Doris was a rather loud, chain-smoking Geordie, in her 80s, who lived directly across the street from our church. She was a lady who was better on your side than against you. I think that is the politest way of describing Doris, and sadly, she took a particular dislike to me. It might have been because I am a Christian pastor, or Welsh, or the portacabin might have had something to do with it. Not sure! Whatever the reason, the best I ever got from Doris was a scowl. Whenever I walked into the local newsagents and Doris was there, the room would go instantly quiet. Then I would get *that* look from her. As much as I felt unnerved by her attitude, I made the decision to treat her with respect and always offered a cheery "Good morning!" though internally I often didn't feel any warmth or goodwill towards her. As a Christian pastor, I attempted to reach out with as much grace as I could muster, and I admit that it was a struggle at times. If she was walking towards me on the pavement, she would always cross the road before she got within 20 yards, and then look the other way, even though I always chose to offer a greeting.

Then one day in early 1996, I saw her coming towards me as I walked to the church from my home. This time, however, she didn't cross the road or look the other way. As usual, I said, "Good morning!" and she replied with "Good morning!" and then gestured towards the building site next to our church where there was some serious building work going on. Doris then declared that she was extremely pleased that we had purchased a row of derelict shops which were an eyesore to the village and were converting them into a community coffee shop. I am not often lost for words, but I was rendered speechless by her comments. This was the first time in over three years that she had responded positively to me. So, I thought I would strike while the iron was hot, and asked her if she would like to don a hard construction hat and come on to the site with me. She immediately said that she would. Doris was someone who liked to be "in the know" and this would have provided her with something to then talk about with her neighbours. Getting to know Doris as I did, I'm sure that she enjoyed having one up on them. I took her from room to room, and explained where everything was going to be, and treated her with as much dignity as if I were showing the bank manager around the place. Doris lapped up the attention. She then promised that when the coffee shop opened, she would visit every day. At that time, I wasn't fully settled in my mind whether that was a good thing or not. It proved to be!

When we opened in October 1996, Doris was there, and visited just about every day until her health finally failed. She offered her services to wash up and help with kitchen duties, popping out every so often for a cigarette. She warmed to the Christian faith, joined our elderly luncheon club, and even occasionally attended our church for specials. Shortly before she passed on, she received Christ as her Lord, and the person who prayed with her was Judith, a local lady who came to faith through an Alpha course that we ran in the Manna House Coffee Shop. Judith, some years later, became the leader of the coffee shop ministry. More about Judith later.

The third element in that equation towards making maximum impact is *clear communication*. Christians really need to remember that we are separated from the New Testament by 2,000 years and 2,000 miles. The New Testament records events in a culture very different from the 21st century Western world. The Old Testament provides a significantly greater challenge as certain books were written closer to 2,500 years ago. It is so, so important to contextualise the Bible and ask what the various Bible passages *meant*, before what they *mean*. That is an absolutely key point if we are going to understand and apply the Bible for today. Whilst the Bible was written *for* us, it wasn't written *to* us. Think about that statement for a moment. It was written by over 40 different authors, in three languages, in three continents, over 600 years (from earlier oral and written accounts) and in a wide range of literary genres, including history, letters (personal and to churches), prophecy, legal documents, poetry, prose, biographies and the apocalyptic writing of Revelation. It wasn't written to us — it was written largely concerning the nation of

Israel and the coming of Israel's Messiah; it was written to real life churches in another age and to individuals — but its genius is that we can draw on its wisdom for our lives and world today. I know of many Christians who just quote the Bible, ignoring the context or genre, leaving their conversation partner in the dark, or should I say, leaving their conversation partner as much in the dark as they are!

Throughout the years, I have attempted to make the message accessible, both in personal witness and in pulpit ministry. I always try to place myself in the shoes of the hearer. In corporate teaching, I ask myself whether an unbeliever of average intelligence will understand what I am teaching. Will that person know my frames of reference? Will they know who Peter, James and John are, let alone Nehemiah or Zerubbabel? I do not assume that everyone present is a mature believer. I so love the wise words of James, brother of Jesus, who told the so-called Jerusalem Council, who met to decide what to do with Gentile converts, that "...we should not make it difficult for the Gentiles who are turning to God" (Acts 15:19). He was speaking about circumcision, but the principle is good for us too. We should do our best to not make it difficult for our visitors who have no knowledge of the Bible. When teaching at church, I try hard to keep in mind the visitor who might not have heard some of these Bible stories before or have any real knowledge of who is who in its pages. Maybe this is best illustrated by American megachurch pastor Andy Stanley. He asks which of the following [exhibits] is the more substantial argument for the resurrection of Jesus from a sceptic's perspective?

> Exhibit A: The Bible says that Jesus rose from the dead after being in the tomb for three days.

> Exhibit B: Matthew, an ex-tax collector who became one of Jesus' followers, writes that Jesus rose from the dead and he claimed to have seen him. Not only that, Luke, a doctor who interviewed eyewitnesses, came to the conclusion that Jesus rose from the dead. He was so convinced that he gave up his practice and became a church-planter. Mark, a friend of the apostle Peter, believed that Jesus rose from the dead based on Peter's account. Peter, the man who denied even knowing Jesus, claimed to have seen the resurrected Christ. Later he was crucified, not for what he believed, but for what he saw:

a resurrected Jesus. James, the brother of Jesus, believed his own brother rose from the dead...[9]

He concludes by saying that we shouldn't believe that Jesus rose from the dead just because the Bible says so. I know that it might sound a little unwieldy, but when I make a reference to some book or character, I most often try to give some context. I don't just claim that "Job said..." but will prefix that by saying something like, "The Old Testament tells a story about a man named Job who lost everything — his health, wealth and family. Some Christians believe that he was an actual historical figure, while others believe that this narrative was an ancient fictional story. That's not the point. The point is what this story tells us about attitudes to suffering..." *etc.* It's so important to be aware of your audience. It is also helpful to try to understand how an unchurched visitor or conversation partner would hear a story for the first time. Let's be honest by saying that some of the Bible stories are a bit weird, even to someone like me who has been a follower of Jesus for over 40 years. I think that as a general rule it's good to address the elephant in the room by acknowledging the strangeness of the story, rather than allow your conversation partner or listener to assume that you think the idea of sacrificing your only son on a mountaintop is acceptable parental behaviour and, worse still, to be willing to do so because that is what God required! I have found it good to emphasise that even one of Jesus' inner circle was renowned for his doubting, and that his brother, James, didn't believe for much of his life, either. It is so easy for people, like me and possibly you, who have been followers of Jesus for a very long time, to forget how strange certain Bible stories might sound to an unbeliever.

---

[9] Stanley, A., *Deep & Wide,* Grand Rapids, Zondervan, 2012, 249.

Dear Lord,

Help us to be real! We confess that our reactions to some situations and some people are not always perfect, but we pray that we will learn to love others as you have loved us.

When we meet people who don't know you yet, please let them see you in us, and give us the wisdom and confidence we need to communicate the good news of Jesus with them. And when it comes to serving you, Lord, please don't let us ever be unwilling to serve in roles which are not centre-stage, if that's where you want us to serve, because we know that every instrument is essential and valued in your kingdom's ensemble of ministries, and through them all you masterfully orchestrate such rich harmonies.

Amen.

From "eyesore" into a hub that became the heart of a community. The Manna House centre was purchased and renovated in 1996. This was a real game-changer for Tamworth Elim Church's community ministry.

CHAPTER TEN

Days of Forming, Days of Filling

IN THE WONDERFUL CREATION NARRATIVE IN GENESIS 1, we are told of how in the beginning God created the heavens and the earth. We are informed of how God just said the word and it came to be. The six days of creation can be divided up into days one to three and days four to six. The first three days are known as days when God formed the earth and the next three days when God filled what he had formed. Day one corresponds to day four, day two to day five, and day three to day six. There is a literary beauty in this chapter which emphasises the orderliness and symmetry of God's creation as the writer of Genesis observes God's order in the earth and heavens.

Within less than four years we had been blessed beyond measure and now had superb community buildings that enabled us to dream dreams of touching the heart of our town. We had experienced the days of forming, and now we were getting ready for the days of filling, or as I have previously mentioned, the jars had all been collected and it was time to start pouring the oil!

Within four years of my taking on the pastorate at Tamworth Elim Church, we moved from being a church with virtually zero community contacts to being a thriving community church. We had a flourishing day nursery that filled the church auditorium from Monday to Friday, a Christian bookshop and community coffee shop with a regular flow of customers. The downside of hosting our day nursery in the main church auditorium was not being able to use the building during weekday nursery hours of 7.30am to 6.00pm, which meant that we needed to borrow the local Methodist church and Anglican church buildings for any funerals. There was one exception: Lily, a lady in her 80s, who had attended the Elim church since she was a child. The thought of hosting her funeral at any other church would have been anathema to her family. On the day of her funeral, we arranged for the entire nursery to go on an outing to a local children's farm for the afternoon. The children spent the morning at the nursery, had lunch, and then were bussed off with most of the staff. A team of volunteers came to dismantle the nursery, which was no mean feat, and set up the church for the funeral, together with musical instruments and PA, and made it look as though all was calm and peaceful for the funeral. Yep, I know what you are thinking: true professionals! To be truthful, behind my composed façade, I was feeling anything other than calm and peaceful! The service went without a hitch, and following the funeral service the room needed to be turned back to a nursery before the kids got back from their outing, only — wait for it! — for it to be dismantled once again, as was the case each Friday evening in preparation for our Sunday services. The Friday dismantling of the day nursery and setting up for church services, and the dismantling of the church after a Sunday service and setting up the day nursery for a Monday, continued for nine long years — emphasis on the *long* — and took its toll on both nursery and church, though we would not have swapped what we had for anything.

With the kind of social outreach ministry that we were employing, it is possible to become impatient, and even disappointed, by lack of results. If you host a large evangelistic campaign in your neighbourhood, with a talented evangelist, you can evaluate the success of your evangelistic outreach almost immediately by the response — whether it be hands raised or those prayed for in some back room by ministry team members, and ultimately those linked into your church or other local churches. However, with such indirect outreach through nurseries and coffee shops, reaping takes longer.

Laurence Singlehurst, in his excellent short book *Sowing, Reaping, Keeping*, tells the story of a country church that had been running a small restaurant in a nearby town.[10] Laurence tells of how the restaurant closed down the day before he visited the church. When he asked the leaders why they had closed the restaurant, they informed him that it had been a failure. Digging a little deeper, he asked them what they meant by failure. Their response was that the restaurant had only witnessed four converts in five years. A conversation ensued.

Laurence asked, "Was the restaurant well used?"

They replied that it was full most days.

---

[10] Singlehurst, L., *Sowing, Reaping, Keeping*, Leicester, Crossway Books, 1995, 23-24.

He then enquired, "How many people do you think, through coming into your restaurant, saw Christians in a more positive light?"

"Oh, thousands," they replied.

He further queried how many people might have viewed God in a more positive light because of their restaurant ministry.

They replied, "Hundreds and hundreds."

Laurence explained that their disappointment and sense of failure came because they had *reaping* expectations of *sowing* strategies. That was an important lesson for us to learn too.

Very early on in our coffee shop ministry we had the joy of introducing a lady named Jenny to Jesus. Jenny was an English teacher in a local high school. She, in fact, taught my children and I had had a few conversations with her through parent evenings at the school and through my working on various committees. Jenny loved the outdoors, and adored horse-riding, show-jumping and motorbikes. She loved the exhilaration and adrenaline rush. Her life was full, and by her own admission, God and church just didn't seem relevant to her, even though she was brought up in a quite traditional Anglican family.

One day, when riding her mare at a local showground, she came down on the last fence. The fall was quite horrendous. Instantaneously, she knew that something serious had happened. She was not wrong. Her spine had snapped at T5 (Thoracic). Jenny was aware of American actor Christopher Reeve, who won a BAFTA Award for his role as Superman, who was left as a quadriplegic after being thrown from a horse during an equestrian competition the previous year, in 1995.[11]

Almost straight away, when Jenny observed the manner in which her legs were splayed, she anticipated that she might not walk again, but what she hadn't bargained for was that she would spend the next ten weeks flat on her back, and the next nine months in a spinal unit in Oswestry, Shropshire. This would have been a torturous period for anyone, let alone someone who had been so active and physically fit as her. As Jenny confessed to me, the scariest thing of all was that she was no longer in control of her life. But she was soon to discover that the God

---

[11] For Jenny's interview with me in at Elim Church on 19th April 2015: the subject was part two in a series entitled 'Where is God when Life Hurts?' (see Tamworth Elim Church podcast) *https://tamworth-elim.org.uk/Media/Player.aspx?media_id=177395& file_id=189554*

that her parents spoke about in their family home when she was a child was the One who would take control of her circumstances and her life.

Jenny's sister, Sarah, was a missionary in Poland with her husband Jeff, and had mobilised her Christian friends worldwide to pray for Jenny. During Jenny's stay in the spinal unit, Sarah invited her to read a book by Joni Eareckson Tada, a Christian author, painter, radio host, singer and advocate for the disabled. Joni, in many ways just like Jenny, lived a very active life in her teens and enjoyed riding horses, swimming and tennis. In 1967, as a 17-year-old, she dived into Chesapeake Bay, misjudging the shallowness of the water, and fractured her spine, resulting in her being paralysed from the shoulders down.

Joni experienced depression, anger, suicidal thoughts and a crisis of faith. During her rehabilitation, she learned to paint by holding the paintbrush between her teeth. She has since authored more than forty books through voice recognition software and has recorded several musical albums. In 1976, she wrote about her experiences in a best-selling autobiography, *Joni: The unforgettable story of a young woman's struggle against quadriplegia and depression.* Given the nature of Joni's story, it is understandable why Jenny was encouraged to read this sad, yet inspiring, story of this amazing Christian lady. But, for Jenny, it was too soon. She was not in a place to read about someone else's life and desperation when she was barely coming to terms with how her own life was going to change beyond anything that she could ever have imagined.

Following Jenny's nine months in the spinal unit, she returned home and became quite depressed. To lift Jenny's spirit, Sarah, who was home from Poland, invited her for a BLT and a mug of hot chocolate with extra dollops of cream and marshmallows — a Manna House special! Jenny hadn't heard of the Manna House, and when Sarah explained where it was, Jenny was even more surprised as she hadn't realised that the former derelict houses were no longer a dilapidated monstrosity but now housed a new and busy community coffee shop.

What happened next was what Jenny refers to as one of those God-incidences in that Julie and I were having lunch at the coffee shop and we went over to speak with her. I had heard that she had had some terrible accident but didn't know of the details. I think that Jenny was a little cautious of me, as we had had divergent views on one of those high school committees. Jenny was a little more liberal in some areas than me. We spoke to Jenny for a little while and then we asked if we could visit her at home. She was very warm to the idea, so that's what we did the following week.

We visited a couple of times and conversation eventually got around to matters of faith. We lent Jenny a great little book entitled *It Makes Sense* by Stephen Gaukroger, a most helpful book on offering some answers to questions that people have on the Christian faith. This seemed to spark an interest in Jenny, and soon she desired to read the Bible for herself. It was approaching Easter, and she was deeply impacted by the love of God, that he should be willing to give his Son, Jesus, to die for the sins of the world, and also Jesus' willingness to suffer on our behalf. It was so wonderful to see Christ's light shine in the darkness of her life and situation, bringing hope where there was despair. Jenny has been a valued member of the church family since then, getting baptised soon after her conversion, which presented the pastors with a few logistical challenges! Jenny has matured into a wonderful example of persevering grace and a person who has real depth to her character. Often Julie and I speak about people like Jenny who have crossed our paths and enriched our lives beyond measure, and by whom we are so incredibly blessed. Oh, by the way, Jenny not only got to read Joni's book but also met her in person at a Spring Harvest Christian festival. I had prearranged with the event organisers for Jenny to meet Joni following her talk one evening. It was a memorable moment for Jenny, and it was memorable for me too. To see these Christian ladies who had so much in common talk as though they were long lost friends and embrace was unforgettable. I'm not ashamed to say that I wiped away a few tears as I observed.

Another such person is Martin who came to faith in Christ just a few months after Jenny. There is no way that I could write a book about our church story without giving mention to Martin, who has been truly God's gift to our church family. Martin is the third of eight children, born to a churchgoing Roman Catholic family in Bradford, Yorkshire. Martin's early experiences of the Christian faith were through the compulsory attendance of church on Sundays and holy days of obligation, enduring mass in Latin, serving as an altar-boy and learning the catechism by rote.

At the age of seventeen, Martin left the family home for college, and thereafter his church attendance was limited to Christmas and Easter when he returned home. Martin's Roman Catholic faith took a back seat for many years, until he and his wife started a family in the late 70s, when two daughters were born. At this time Martin picked up the traditions of his childhood. Both his daughters were christened as babies and were taken along to church with him when they were old enough to join in, but once they reached their teenage years they opted out, which demotivated Martin, causing him to relapse into occasional seasonal attendance.

Roll on several years to Easter 1997. Martin's elder daughter came home from university for the Easter break and expressed a desire to attend a service at a Pentecostal church. Martin had no idea what a Pentecostal church was, or what they believed, or indeed where he might find such a place. He needed to look this up in the *Yellow Pages* — this was pre-Google! — to discover whether there were any Pentecostal churches nearby. There was, and we spoke on the phone about the times of our Sunday services. Martin and his daughter attended our Easter Service the following Sunday.

I'll allow Martin to share his own thoughts about his first visit:

To say this was a revelation is understating the matter. No liturgy, no candles, no hymns, no special vestments, simply a small congregation of people who were clearly and profoundly aware of the love of God in their lives and a teaching session from the pastor which focused on the boundless grace of Christ. This was a revelation. Instead of the familiar sense of unworthiness and urgent call for repentance, I was made aware of the gift of love and life, paid in full by the blood of Christ.

Martin's daughter returned to university, but Martin felt drawn to return week after week to learn more about this new and intriguing expression of Christian faith. Martin acknowledges:

I spent many Sunday services in the back row, struggling (and failing) to hold back my tears, as unbeknown to me at the time, many around me prayed for me to come to faith.

Martin and I met on Monday evenings for coffee and cake in my church office for a few months to allow Martin to explore matters of faith and to deepen his understanding. His younger daughter, who was studying for her A-levels at the time, also joined us. They were fascinating conversations held with two very intelligent people. To say that they kept me on my toes would be an understatement!

At this time, Martin was working as a director in a multinational company which caused him to work overseas quite a lot, and sometimes

I would receive a call on some aspect of theology at all sorts of hours of day and night. God was working very powerfully in his life, and I remember on 12th June 1997, Martin, having just come back from a trip to the USA, rang me from his office.

"Steve, can I come over to meet you?" he asked.

"Yes, come now," I responded.

He walked through my office door and fell on his knees to receive Christ. Little did I know when I first met Martin that he would become someone who would serve the purposes of God so passionately and who would help shape the vision and values of Tamworth Elim Church for over two decades.

In fact, he was so passionate for Jesus that I worried that he would burn himself out. I said to him on a few occasions, "Life is a marathon, not a 100 metres sprint!" I needn't have concerned myself as the pace that Martin set at the beginning as a 48-year-old new Christian is the same pace that he continues to run with today as a 69-year-old.

Martin is a man of great integrity, spirituality, compassion and amazing ability, and although he "does not have any formal theological training or an ecclesiastical ordination, my wife Julie refers to Martin as her 'pastor' and I doubt that she is alone in doing so"[12].

Over the years, Martin has used skills and capabilities honed by his time in industry. He wrote to me recently, "Over the years I have come to know the challenges, the joys and the fullness of the Christian life, and to deeply know the grace of God that knows no limits. I am also happy to claim that I found God — or rather, He found me — in the *Yellow Pages!*"

Just a quick word to all church leaders: that person who has made a casual enquiry about your church, who has a multitude of questions about the Christian faith, who might have baggage of religious traditions that hinder rather than help him or her reach out to Jesus, might, in time, become your right-hand man or woman for years to come in your church. Why not ask the Lord to give you grace-filled eyes to see what people might become, rather than where they start?

---

[12] These are words I used in my Foreword for his book of poetry: Wild, M., *The Gospels in Harmony*, Exeter, Onwards and Upwards Publishers, 2018.

Dear Lord,

Help us to keep sowing seeds of your love, kindness and compassion into our communities. Thank you that the light of your love shines brightest through the darkest of circumstances and you bring hope in times of deepest despair. We are constantly in awe of the way you transform lives and we delight in those special people who cross our path and journey with us a while. What a blessing they are!

Thank you, Lord!

Amen.

Jenny — one of many people who have crossed our paths and enriched our lives beyond measure.

Chapter Eleven

Man Plans and God Laughs!

VERY FEW OF THE FIFTY OR SO ORIGINAL CONGREGATION IN 1992, when I was welcomed as pastor, are still with us on the journey. Some have moved away, some have been "promoted" to heaven and some, sadly, are no longer walking the journey of faith. That continues to sadden me deeply.

One of the originals is a lady named Jan, a gregarious and larger-than-life lady, with a beaming smile and a big heart. Jan had been attending the church for about five years before our arrival. Fairly early on in my ministry, Jan made a decision to be baptised by full immersion, as is our practice. This, for her, was a big step as she had been brought up in a church tradition where she had been baptised as a child. Given her earlier church background and teaching, she had understandably, and for a long time, resisted a subsequent "believer's" baptism. Whilst Jan's baptism on 4th July 1993 was questioned by some members of her family, it proved to be a significant turning point in her Christian journey.

That step of faith, I believe, was an important act of obedience to the Lord, and prepared her for making the next, much larger, stride forward in days to come. That is often the way that the Lord works in our lives. He never seems to ask us to run before we can walk, and the lesser areas of obedience often come before the more significant asks.

Jan got more involved in church life and started taking greater interest in what was going on in church between Sundays, especially in the community outreach of the Manna House project, which commenced in 1996. At that time Jan was working in a local bank and expected to be working there until her normal retirement age. She had worked her way up from part-time cashier to assistant manager in just seven years. However, there is an old Yiddish adage, *"Mann tracht, und Gott lacht,"* which means, "Man plans, and God laughs." Despite our most careful planning, the twists and turns in our life's journey can, and do, surprise us. This is especially so when we cry out to God and ask that he will use us in some way, as Jan did in one of our services. If you sincerely pray for God to use you, as she did, then hold on to your hat!

When Jan returned home, following her promise to serve the Lord, she opened a Christian magazine and was confronted by an advert to train as a Christian counsellor. As she read the advert, something stirred in her heart. She wrestled with the thought of this, not getting much sleep that night. The following day she spoke to a friend from our church who worked as a hospital counsellor and asked if he had ever heard of the counselling institution that advertised in the Christian magazine. He laughed, and then confirmed that this was how he started his counselling career, and encouraged Jan to enrol.

Jan studied via a correspondence course for six months before enrolling on a further course to learn about bereavement work. It was there, in discussion with other Christian counsellors, that she was inspired with the idea of a Christian counselling service running from our Manna House community buildings. She then spoke with her house group friends who encouraged her to come and chat with me. She made an appointment and came with the intention of asking whether she would be able to help someone to set up such a service at the Manna House. She brought various pamphlets and brochures to the meeting to support her case but had no idea of what was coming! I was so impressed by her vision, passion and obvious ability, as well as the potential for bringing spiritual and emotional health to those hurt through life's turmoil and trials, that I said to her, "Sounds great. Get on with it then!" If she had known how I was going to respond, I don't think that she would ever have had the courage to ask for a meeting in the first place! Looking back over the last twenty or so years, at the date of writing, my expectations of her have been justified. Although her initial desire was to help support someone else, I cannot think of a better advocate and front-person to what has been an amazing ministry.

Following our meeting, Jan did some research with the Association of Christian Counsellors, took the decision to leave her career — her work colleagues thought she'd gone mad! — and started a counselling service on her own in January 1998, with the support and encouragement of our church leaders. Within months, God brought other counsellors alongside Jan to serve Jesus through serving the needs of those who were often lost and without hope in this world. In the hay-day of the counselling service we had twenty counsellors, not only serving our immediate community, but also taking on literally hundreds of referrals from local GP surgeries. This was funded by the local Primary Care Trust. It has been wonderfully inspiring to witness broken lives being restored, with many later coming to faith. However, funding from the Trust ceased some thirteen years later, and we needed to downscale our service to where it started — Jan.

To witness the counselling service diminish in this way was hugely disappointing from a human perspective, but we have learned through the years, there are seasons for everything, as the author of Ecclesiastes writes:

> *There is a time for everything,*
> *and a season for every activity under the heavens:*
> *a time to be born and a time to die,*
> *a time to plant and a time to uproot...*

Ecclesiastes 3:1-2

There are times of sowing and also times of reaping, a time to plant a new ministry and a time to uproot that ministry, a time for ministries to be born and a time for them to die — God's time. There are seasons when God sets up ministry opportunities, and there are seasons when God draws a line and brings that term to an end. As Job said, "The LORD gave and the LORD has taken away; may the name of the LORD be praised" (Job 1:21). The context of those words was when Job lost his health, wealth and family in a disastrous chain of events, but the principle still remains: the Lord gives and the Lord takes away. Our challenge during these times is to say as Job said, "May the name of the Lord be praised."

We were disappointed with the counselling service shrinking in its reach, but through Jan this ministry has continued to bless others, from inside and outside the church. She has been unrelenting in using her God-given expertise to bring healing to over one hundred clients since serving this ministry on her own again. Jan recognises that her work is to use her skills for God and by his empowering. As she often says to me, "He is the ultimate healer, not me. I'm just his tool." I couldn't disagree with that!

We, at Tamworth Elim, have learned not to hold on too tightly to ministries, and that a closed door is as much an answer from God as an open door. I would certainly rather the Lord would close a door that is meant to be closed than I would attempt to keep a door open, by human effort and ingenuity, that is no longer God's desire and will. We suffer from bruised fingers when God needs to prise open our hands because we are holding too tightly to something that he doesn't want us to hold on to anymore.

It would be incomplete to write of our counselling service and not mention two other outreaches closely associated with the Manna House counselling ministry — our Pregnancy Crisis Centre and Evaluate. In 1999, the year following the commencement of the counselling service, we started a Pregnancy Crisis Centre in our Manna House community buildings, where women and girls came for pregnancy tests, an opportunity to discuss the options if the pregnancy was unwanted, and miscarriage and post-abortion counselling. We set up the Pregnancy Crisis Centre in association with CARE, a Christian charity involved in a wide range of social and family ministries. To become a CARE centre we required a minimum of ten people to set it up. We could have drummed up that kind of support from our own church, but we believed that this should be an outreach project owned by the combined churches of Tamworth. When asking other churches in our town if there were any interested in this work of pregnancy crisis, we had exactly ten volunteers. What a lovely God-incidence!

Over the years, we have set up a range of community projects under the banner of the Manna House which have involved volunteers and leaders from other Tamworth churches. These include Manna House Counselling, Pregnancy Crisis Centre, Foodbank and a separate Tam-worth-based charity called The Starfish Project, which started as an outreach to those affected by drugs and their families, though over the years the remit of this charity has extended to be a catch-all ministry to those on the margins of society. More recently, we have added a winter night shelter to the outreach of The Starfish Project, providing a hot meal, a warm bed and friendship to our town's rough sleepers during the three coldest months of the year. Whilst this is not a perfect solution to this need, we join with six other churches to provide this service in our various church buildings and halls. Ideally, a central shelter would be better, running throughout the year with a salaried staff, but for now, something is better than nothing. We at Elim have such an excellent team led by Tina and her daughters Carrie and Abby.

One of our "gifts" to our fellow Christians of other denominations throughout Tamworth has been our ability to move quickly with new projects, such as the Pregnancy Crisis Centre. Basically, this is largely due to our church governance, which is essentially Presbyterian.[13] Our church is led through an appointed eldership team who seek God for his direction. Because we are governed by a team of elders, we aren't required to get permission from either some bureaucratic hierarchy or even from our church members. Essentially, the church eldership seeks God on church vision, and then moves forward in faith when it senses it has heard God's mandate or direction. I am fully aware that a danger of this form of church government is "heavy shepherding" or spiritual bullying, where leaders become overbearing and dogmatic. Therefore, it is imperative that it is tempered by humility and servant-hearted leadership. It must also be said that if a leader thinks he is leading but no one is following, all he is actually doing is going out for a walk! Think about that one! One of our church's mottos is, "The greatest you can become in the kingdom of God is a servant." Anyone who has been a part of our church family for more than a couple of months will have heard that saying.

Thankfully, our church family is perfectly at ease in following the vision and direction of the church eldership team. This change in attitude took place following the success of our purchasing, renovating and refurbishing the former derelict eyesore of our community into the Manna House centre, even though at that time some of our church family thought it was a ridiculous venture which was doomed to fail. Mercifully, we heard from God correctly, and as "ridiculous" as that project was for a small church, we succeeded and thereafter won favour from the people. The amazing thing is that, after that first major victory of faith, the church family has trusted the leadership team on all future major decisions, which in itself is a benefit of creating a culture of transparency and openness. There is a general acceptance that the church is led well by godly leaders, whose desire is to lead the church family into better places.

Let's return to the Pregnancy Crisis Centre. Many of our clients thought of abortion as the easy option to an unwanted pregnancy. Some had made up their minds even before visiting the centre. Others were open to advice and help from our skilled, wonderfully compassionate team, who provided other alternatives, including adoption, in a non-judgemental environment. It was always a delight to our staff when such a baby or child was later introduced to them who might not have been

---

[13] For a study on the various types of church governance: Ericksen, M., *Christian Doctrine,* Grand Rapids, Baker, 1998, 1070-1082.

born had it not been for the counselling service. Jan remembers dancing around the room with exhilaration after receiving a phone call from a lady who told her that as she spoke, she was holding a beautiful little girl in her arms, and only because she came into the Pregnancy Crisis Centre and was helped to make the right choice. One young girl who came to the centre for a pregnancy test made the decision to abort. Her mother, a Christian believer, vehemently disagreed with her views, but felt that she needed to support her daughter's decision and chose to go with her to the clinic where the termination was to take place. On the journey to the clinic, the mother, who was driving the car, was required to stop at a pedestrian crossing as a young mother and her child crossed the road in front of them. This simple moment acted like a catalyst to the pregnant girl. Something touched her deeply in seeing that mother and child. Immediately, she asked her mother to turn around and go home, and that she had changed her mind about the termination, much to the relief of her mother and as an answer to prayer. For several years, that girl was a regular attender of our church, alongside her parents, grandparents and later a younger brother and sister. She was a living reminder of the importance of the pregnancy crisis work.

With the increasing numbers of young girls coming into our Pregnancy Crisis Centre, we realised that, if possible, it would be better for us to teach them about life's risks rather than to sort out their problems later. As the old saying goes, it is better to put a fence at the top of the cliff than have a hospital at the bottom. We had no intention of getting rid of the "hospital" but we were minded to erect the fence at the top. This commenced with lessons on pregnancy in a local high school after being encouraged by a Christian teacher who taught there. Soon after this work commenced, we were introduced to a new national programme from CARE, called Evaluate, aimed at helping young people make wise decisions in areas of sex and relationships through relevant and interactive multimedia presentations, seeking to empower young people to make healthy and informed choices, and delaying sexual experience until in a committed relationship, ideally marriage.

A team of six able communicators plus technical support staff were trained to provide essential sex and relationships teaching for high school children, thus enabling students to have an awareness of media influence and peer-pressure, teaching them about drugs and alcohol and their effect on decision-making, and imparting knowledge about pregnancy, sexually-transmitted infections and contraception. This programme seemed to tick all the boxes for schools on their Personal, Social and Health Education (PSHE) programmes. The team practised their programme every week to provide an engaging presentation. After all, you only have one opportunity to make a first impression, and the impression that they made on many schools was excellent. The team became accredited by CARE and presented this important message to over 5,000 young people in ten high schools within our locality. The feedback from students and teachers was massively positive. Unfortunately, with education cutbacks the funding for this programme ran out. Whilst our team gave freely of their time and raised funding to purchase all the equipment — including a laptop, video projector, sound equipment, screen and microphones — a non-negotiable franchise fee per student was also required. In addition to the extra finance that was required to keep this programme on the road, the strain was beginning to show on the team due to the need to practise weekly and then deliver presentations in various high schools, the substantial administration of the programme, and lastly the not insignificant need to negotiate time off from work for those with regular employment. That said, we praise God for all that was accomplished through this opportunity to speak to so many young people.

Before I move on, let me share one last story of our pregnancy crisis ministry. Leanne (not her real name) had no idea when she took her first spliff that it would lead to years of addiction. She was only 14 when she was introduced to cannabis, shortly before she became a mum for the first time. Just four days after her daughter was born, Leanne's father died of a heart attack at the age of 37, which she claimed was the trigger that pushed her towards harder drugs — first amphetamines and then heroin. She was told that heroin would take away all her problems, emotions, pain and anger. The dealers gave it to her for free for the first three weeks, which was the length of time it took to get addicted. Heroin became her world and it dictated what she could do and what she could not do each day. She even confessed that she put heroin before her little girl, and as soon as she woke up in the morning, it was heroin that she reached for first.

Life continued downhill, and at the age of 18, Leanne was pregnant for the second time after an abusive relationship. Through her mother's church, she was introduced to our Manna House Pregnancy Crisis Centre, which in turn helped her make the decision to release her baby for adoption. Jan helped her through the process and also introduced her to Teen Challenge, a Christian-based drug rehabilitation centre. Referring to the adoption, Leanne said, "It wasn't a decision I made easily but I was already a single mum addicted to heroin. I couldn't love myself let alone two children, so I decided to put my son first and give him the best start in life. The day I handed my son over was one of the hardest days of my life. However, the adoptive parents were lovely and I couldn't have wished for anyone better." Through her mum's influence and through this painful process, Leanne heard of Jesus and how he could set her free. She received his life-transforming love, a decision that changed her life. She claims that the 16-month programme at Teen Challenge was exceptionally difficult, yet was one of the best and most worthwhile things she ever did. For the first time in her life, she started to love and respect herself. Her physical appearance changed: she went from being a scraggy six stones to weighing in at a healthy ten stones. Leanne was later happily married and became a loving and caring mother.

Eventually, after a number of years, the pregnancy crisis work was no longer necessary because senior schools "upped their game" and provided better support for young girls through pregnancy testing and counselling. It was sad to see an end to this work, but we continue to look back with fond memories and thank God for his grace to us throughout this ministry.

When we speak of our spiritual journey and many community ministries, we often refer to it in terms of having a number of rooms joined together. The only way to enter these rooms is to enter through the front door of the first room. At the rear of the first room there is another door which leads to the second room. Once in the second room there is another door at the rear which leads to the third room *etc.* That was our story: we obeyed what God was showing us at that moment only to be presented with another door of opportunity at some future point. Had we not taken that initial step of faith, the second, third or fourth doors would not have presented themselves to us.

Dear Lord,

We are grateful for your guidance and amazed that you choose to use us to make Earth a little more like Heaven.

Thank you for all the people who use their skills and talents to help others, and in doing so, not only show them a better way to live, but also point them to Jesus. We are truly thankful for the people you have put in place to help us when we've been in need, and for those who introduced us to you, Lord.

Out of the fullness of our gratitude, help us to serve you wholeheartedly. We ask that you open our eyes to see the doors you are opening before us, and that you give us the faith to walk through.

Amen.

CHAPTER TWELVE

Outgrowing Our Facilities

SINCE ITS INCEPTION IN 1996, THE MANNA HOUSE CENTRE has become a halfway house for people who had no contact with the church to meet with Christians outside a formal church setting. I imagine that if more people without a church background or connection had an opportunity to meet with Christians in a more neutral context, they might be less fearful of entering through the front door of a church building every now and again. Those who came through the doors of our coffee shop, bookshop, Pregnancy Crisis Centre or for counselling were often won over by kindness and grace. They were always made to feel welcome, were shown compassion and were always given a listening ear. It didn't take too long before they realised that Christians don't have two heads and most are nothing like Bible-quoting Dot Cotton from East-enders!

Over the next few years our church congregation started growing. By 2000, the Sunday congregation had doubled from the church that I had inherited some eight years previously. Each Sunday, there were over 100 people in attendance, alongside a busy Sunday School. I cannot remember any event or specific occasion when the church grew. We never had an influx of new Christians or new families wishing to join our church. Our growth was more like the imperceptible growth of that pre-school niece who is certainly taller than she was in last year's holiday photos though the child's growth would go unnoticed by those constantly around her. Our chief concern at Elim was to create a healthy church; and healthy churches, just like healthy children, grow naturally.

However, by the start of the new millennium we needed to think about how we were going to accommodate our growing congregation. It is well attested that churches will not grow beyond 80% of their seating capacity. The reason for this is that couples, families, or for that matter friends, wish to sit next to each other at church. For example, if a visiting family of two adults and their three kids turn up at church at 10.30am and can only be seated by two younger children sitting with mum on the front row, and with dad and the older child needing to find seats elsewhere in the building, you probably won't see them again!

A full church wasn't our only "problem". We also needed space for our day nursery to call its own. For the previous nine years the nursery had used our main church auditorium, which was awkward for both the nursery and for the church. We also required a larger industrial kitchen and extra space to commence a new outreach to socially isolated older people.

We needed to think of ways to extend our buildings, and how we could pay for it. We had spoken to a firm of specialist church architects, who drew us some plans in exchange for a fee that made us grimace. The local planning department didn't want to know and point blank refused to even discuss the concept that the architects had worked on. There were lessons to be learned.

We were left without a contingency and no money in the bank, but still needed to move forward in our plans and thinking. As the saying goes, "Once bitten, twice shy!" and in the light of our previous architectural costs we were going to be a little more cautious next time around. I've always had a "can do" attitude to most things in life, and didn't believe that drawing architectural plans was going to be rocket science. So, for a few months in early 2001, I burned the midnight oil and drew some plans for a church extension. The plans, if I say it myself, were quite spectacular and were aimed at linking the Manna House charity buildings and the church building on three storeys. It was easy enough measuring the floor plan, but to work out the heights of the buildings to provide elevations was much more challenging. I had an ingenious thought: I would count bricks. If one brick equals so many millimetres, then I could fairly easily work out building heights and the various elevations for the building. So that's what I did!

Unlike the previous attempt by the church architectural specialists, I had a continuing dialogue with the planning department. Doing it this way prevented us from having a nasty surprise of being refused planning permission after spending many thousands of pounds in fees. After several months of dialogue, the borough planning department was quite happy to recommend my plans, though our neighbours, not surprisingly, were less than happy. To be fair, I could see why they were so upset. Our buildings would prevent them seeing a sunset ever again and perhaps cause them a severe dose of claustrophobia. But we didn't have too many options. This appeared to be the only way forward to be able to house our growing congregation. As ever, the planners never have the last word on planning matters. That responsibility rests with the elected members of the council who sit on the planning committee who either accept or reject the planners' recommendations. For several weeks, the councillors had their ears bent by locals about this monstrosity of a building that the Elim Church was wishing to build and were told of all the ways that building would be detrimental to their lives. There were times that I entertained the idea of wearing body armour and a tin hat to walk to my office on a morning. To put it mildly, I wasn't the first name on their Christmas card list!

The local newspaper, that had always been a supporter of our community ministry, reported accurately on the proposed building plans with double page spreads. They were simply doing their job, and doing it well, but such publicity just helped to raise the temperature to boiling point. Neighbours were worried about increased traffic; "bigger church buildings" equals "bigger congregations" equals "more traffic" in a residential area that already had too many cars. Bamford Street, where our church is located, is a narrow street with houses dating back to the late 1800s. It was a street that was never intended for *any* cars, let alone two cars per property as is the case nowadays.

The evening for the planning meeting at the council offices arrived. A small pocket of people from the church attended to listen to proceedings. I was invited to give a five-minute speech in support of our application, which I did. I found the occasion nowhere as easy as speaking on matters of faith to our Sunday congregation. This was uncomfortable. Actually, it was hostile. Our three immediate neighbours whose houses backed on to our church land, and who would have been most affected by these buildings, treated us as the enemy, with icy stares and whispers that were meant to be overheard. The case was heard fairly, but our planning application was turned down. The mood of our neighbours lightened instantly, and as they vacated the building there were handshakes and even a certain amount of back-slapping. My mood wasn't so elated. I was so glad that none of my church friends thought it wise to tell me that "God works all things together for good" just at that moment. Wise indeed. I'm not sure how I would have reacted. Whilst I believe that God has a wonderful knack of turning negatives into positives, I wouldn't have been ready to hear it just then. So I said, "Goodnight," went home and watched a detective drama whilst enjoying a couple of glasses of red wine. I find both helpful to unwind. Each to his own!

A few days later our eldership team met to discuss what to do next. One option was to take our council to tribunal. There was a lot to be said for challenging them in the courts as, after all, the borough planning department — the "professionals" — had said yes to our application. The councillors, whose decision it was, had said no for expediency and political reasons. Since we did not have any contingency plans, it seemed the wisest and most natural thing to do — challenge them at tribunal.

However, the more our leaders spoke about the possibility of taking on the council at a legal tribunal, the more we felt repulsed by the idea. There was a very real sense of what I imagine the early believers felt at the first church council in Jerusalem when they discussed what to do with Gentile believers. Were these non-Jews expected to become Jewish before being accepted as members of the church? What about their dietary requirements? What about circumcision? The council in Jerusalem agreed on a way forward, not requiring the Gentiles to be circumcised and releasing them from needing to follow a long list of Jewish rituals. They concluded by saying that their decision "seemed good to the Holy Spirit and us" (Acts 15:28). Following our meeting that evening, we also said that our decision not to challenge the council over their refusal of planning permission "seemed good to the Holy Spirit and us". In fact, we were convinced that if we had taken the council to tribunal, we would be fighting against God himself. This, pragmatically, was a hard decision to come to as we did not have any alternatives. It really was a matter of going back to the drawing board, in our case literally.

As I've said previously, it isn't always easy to hear God's direction clearly, yet there are those occasions when we have greater clarity, times when we know that a certain course of action is wrong, and we have no sense of *shalom* — that deep sense of well-being of soul. This was one of those occasions. In time, we were able to see some of the reasons why this wasn't God's way forward for us.

Roll on a few months. I was standing in the church car park, with sketchpad in hand, attempting to imagine how we could extend our buildings in this very densely populated area, making sure that we did not infringe on our neighbours' privacy with buildings overlooking gardens and casting dark shadows over their properties, while at the same time creating buildings that didn't take away many of our precious car spaces, which were pure gold dust. I was deep in thought when Judith, a local lady who had recently come to faith, passed by.

Judith and I engaged in conversation about our prospective building plans. Rather nonchalantly, she informed me that her husband, Bob, was an architect and he would be only too happy to help with our plans and that it would not cost us the earth. Food for thought! But before chatting to Bob I knew that I needed to get a handle on what the buildings needed to look like as no one knew better than me how the new buildings would actually function.

I spent some more weeks drawing sketches of the shape and size of the buildings and the ways that the space would be divided into rooms, kitchens, offices, toilets and corridors, especially in our new bespoke day nursery on two storeys that would offer 64 places to babies and pre-school children. Bob then took my amateur sketches and turned them into proper architectural plans, occasionally informing me that there was some legal reason why we couldn't follow all my ideas.

The plans were submitted and accepted by the borough planning department in January 2002. As usual, there were some who objected to what we were trying to do, but this time there wasn't the support from local council members that our opponents had on the previous occasion. There seemed to be a different atmosphere and a greater willingness to run with this latest scheme, and so it proved. The planning subcommittee of our local council met to discuss the recommendations of their planning department. I spoke for five minutes as previously, there was a short discussion among the councillors and a decision was made. Approval!

Yes, approval! I wanted to do cartwheels across the room, but refrained from doing so and did my best not to over-celebrate or gloat. I was a bit like a footballer who has just scored the winning goal against his former club. The footballer who would normally celebrate by running to the corner flag, performing the actions of the Birdie Song, or by making some other obtuse gesture, but out of respect for his former team mates and fans he quietly jogs back to the halfway line and plays down his achievement. I was quite proud of myself for behaving so impeccably.

Alongside the committee's planning approval, we were elated to hear a planning councillor thank us for not taking the council to tribunal on the previous occasion. We appreciated his gesture, but that comment in itself was an indication of how tenuous they believed their earlier rejection to be. I went home, made a few phone calls to share the good news with those I knew had been praying for us, and then celebrated with a couple of glasses of red wine and a detective drama on the box! Okay! Okay! I know what you are thinking!

Two days later, Bob, our architect, asked to speak with me. We met at my office, and after initial pleasantries, Bob asked me to pray for him as he wished to receive Christ. I was ecstatic and praised God that he not only brought Bob to himself, but also provided me with such a lovely confirmation that we had done the right thing in not challenging the council at tribunal, and that our present plans were those that had God's approval. If God was in this, then I also believed that he would supply the finance required to fund this project.

Lord,

Thank you for delivering us from ourselves, from our imperfect plans and less-than-ideal ideas! We are prone to rest easily in the knowledge that you always want what is best for us, but fail to acknowledge that you have that same desire for everyone, including those who oppose us. You have no favourites! All we ask, Lord, is that you continue to lead us in your ways, that we might truly see "your kingdom come here, as in Heaven".

Help us to be confident in upholding those things that "seem good to the Holy Spirit and to us". We rejoice in your willingness to give us so much more than we could ever imagine.

Amen.

CHAPTER THIRTEEN

Becoming Foolish for Christ

A COUPLE OF MONTHS LATER, I ATTENDED AN ANNUAL conference hosted by the Elim Church. Each year, all church ministers and lay leaders are required to attend a business conference which provides the legal governance of our Movement. Apart from needing to deal with constitutional matters, the conference is an opportunity to receive ministry from various church leaders and hear of some of the good things happening in our Movement. I, along with a few others, was invited to say a few words about our community development and ministry in one ministerial session. Following my talk, Lyndon Bowring, the Executive Director of CARE, spoke to me to say that he was encouraged by what we were attempting to do in Tamworth. Lyndon is a terrific guy who was a guest lecturer when I was a first-year student at Elim Bible College. He was everyone's favourite — a man with passion, vision, wisdom and a wonderful sense of humour. For many years, he had been serving God in the corridors of power, leading an organisation that provided a Christian voice on ethical matters in Parliament. Lyndon was also a minister ordained by Elim and remained on the staff of Kensington Temple, which was the largest Pentecostal church in Europe at that time.

I informed Lyndon that we were planning a further expansion of our church and community buildings, intending to add extra office space, an industrial kitchen, a new annexe to the church, a self-contained 64-place day nursery and an extended worship auditorium on our church, doubling its size to 240. Lyndon, as ever, was massively encouraging and interested in what we were doing. I thought I would strike while the iron was hot, and asked Lyndon to come and speak at our opening event when the buildings were built. I also explained that we had up to five years to get the work started, and that the cost of this project would be in the region of £500k. It was actually closer to £800k! I also informed him that we didn't have any money saved up at the time and that our congregation wasn't especially wealthy — the inference being, this won't happen soon, so he didn't need to cancel his summer holidays that year!

One afternoon in June 2002, I sat in my office contemplating prayerfully over the future of our extension, when I was reminded of the story of the Levites who were tasked with carrying the Ark of the Covenant from the desert where they had been encamped for 40 years into the land that God had promised the nation of Israel. To get to their place of inheritance they needed to get past the flooded River Jordan. We are told in Joshua 3 that as soon as they placed their feet in the Jordan, the waters parted, just as the Red Sea had parted 40 years previously when the Israelites escaped the Egyptians.

The lesson I believe God was teaching me was that the Levitical priests, in faith, needed to place their feet in the river before the waters parted. It is a bit like those electric supermarket doors that open when you walk close enough to the sensor. If you stand back, the doors will remain closed. I immediately knew what this image of the Levites was all about. The Lord was showing me that I needed to move forward and take some action before I would see the fulfilment of the vision. Further to knowing that I needed to take some action, I knew — I just *knew* — what I was required to do. I cannot say that I often get these special moments of revelation. I've probably only ever had a handful of such occasions when I was given some clear supernatural revelation in this manner in over 40 years of following Jesus. But on this occasion, I believed that I had heard from God.

So, what was he requiring me to do?

Wait for it... I believed that he wanted me to make contact with Lyndon again and ask if he would provide a date for speaking at the grand opening of our church and community buildings the following year — that is, in mid-2003. Let's stop there for a moment. It was already June 2002 and the project was going to cost, I believed at the time, a massive £500k. I knew that if I had got this wrong, then I was going to look very, very foolish indeed. I didn't mind becoming a "fool for Christ" (1 Cor. 4:10) but I wasn't thrilled about being just *plain* foolish. There is a difference. There was an occasion as a fairly new Christian when I did something very foolish in my own strength and not in God's strength. The result was that I was embarrassed and hurt, and the shame of that moment lived with me for a long time after; even today, some 40 years on, I still get hot flushes of embarrassment over my foolhardiness. You are probably asking what on earth I did. I'll tell you but try not to laugh too loudly!

I had just become a science student at Cardiff University, and along with other members of the class was required to stand and give a ten-minute presentation in front of a camera and to the rest of the class. Quite cutting edge in those days! As a very new Christian, with lots of passion but zero wisdom, I thought I would use this opportunity to preach at them. In those days I was a bit of a fundamentalist and I thought that a bit of hell-fire preaching would do them no harm at all. I even envisaged myself being invited to go from place to place sharing my testimony of how students and lecturers came to faith through my "obedience" to God. Worse still, I had been reading some awful dispensationalist material in an American paperback on the Second Coming of Christ, and used that material unthinkingly! The class didn't fall on their knees in deep repentance. They just laughed — and laughed very loudly. I can still see the lecturers doing their best to keep a straight face, as I got redder and redder in the face, and truly wanted the Second Coming to happen that second. It was awful, and I deserved everything I got in that lecture room that day. I was laughed out of the room! If you were one of the lecturers or students, I want you to know that I've become a bit more normal since then. Over the years, you might have even told that story to your friends over a beer or two, and yourself wondered what had happened to that fresh-faced, fundamentalist Wally who tried to dangle you over the pit of hell — well, now you know! Please forgive my foolishness.

Needless to say, I did not want Lyndon to laugh as loudly over my letter as my former student colleagues had that day, but I was neverthe-less convinced that it was God who had placed in my heart the idea to make contact with him.

With a deep breath and trust in God, I wrote the following:

26th June 2002.

Dear Lyndon,

It was a pleasure to meet you at this year's Elim Conference. Your words to me later that day were a great encouragement. Thank you.

I know that much water has passed under the bridge since then, but I asked on that occasion if you would speak at an opening of an extension of our church and community facilities, once built. You kindly agreed.

We have received full planning permission for a four phase extension costing in the region of £500,000. This will provide us with a kitchen extension, extra office, community rooms, a day nursery for 66 children and an extension of 140 seats on our church building.

Presently, we do not have any guaranteed finance. However, and I know that this sounds extremely wacky, I believe that we can raise the finance and even finish building by this time next year. With this in mind, would it be possible for you to provide me (provisionally) a Saturday and Sunday in May or June 2003? If this is OK with you, perhaps I could give you an update on things later in the year? At least by that time I will know whether the strict timetable is feasible. If not, perhaps you would be willing to reschedule for later in the year?

Lyndon, I should like to take this opportunity to thank you for your ministry which has been a significant blessing to evangelical believers throughout the UK and especially to our church in Tamworth. I personally have the highest regard for what you do, for what CARE stands for, and the resources it provides. Thank you. The whole ethos of our church is to make an impact within our community for Christ, which I believe we have in measure achieved. Although we are a relatively small church, we now run a day nursery for 36 children, have special needs accommodation for three people, have a counselling service and a Pregnancy Crisis Centre (linked to Care for Life), a community coffee and bookshop, a salaried schools worker and a host of other church based activities. All of these ministries have emerged over the last eight years. Incidentally, our vision for the Pregnancy Crisis Centre is to present the message on the sanctity of life to every pupil in all the secondary schools in Tamworth. We are presently halfway there, now being invited into three of the six secondary schools in the town on a regular basis.

Thanks for taking the time to read this letter. Look forward to hearing from you...

The message was sent by snail mail. One week later, Lyndon telephoned me to talk about my letter, saying that he would love to come to Tamworth and be our speaker in the Grand Opening of our new church and community buildings. He got it! He knew that my correspondence was a step of faith, and he wanted to join me in that step. We added a date in our diaries for May 2003; I thanked him and told him I would be in touch, hopefully soon.

What happened next was quite remarkable. Within a few weeks we started receiving cheques — big cheques, cheques from trust funds and promises of money from central government. £10k one day, then £56k, then £20k, then £152k, then another £10k, then another £56k *etc.* — in total £440,000 was donated to us. Yes, I had worked jolly hard in writing applications (many weeks topped 80 hours) to many charitable foundations and others whom I thought might be able to help fund this mammoth project, but until that joint step of faith with Lyndon, we were not promised a penny. I've often thought about that time and can only explain it in terms of living under an open heaven. Something spiritual happened when Lyndon and I stepped into the flooded Jordan. The original date for the Grand Opening was moved back to May 2004, but that was not even slightly significant to us. The Lord was teaching us once again that he is no man's debtor and remains faithful in all things. I've often challenged the Tamworth Elim family that you will never walk on water unless you're prepared to get out of the boat, a reference to Peter stepping out of the boat one stormy night in the middle of the Sea of Galilee at Jesus' command.

———————————

Dear Lord,

We can be so foolish at times! Forgive us for rushing in where angels fear to tread! Forgive us too, Lord, for being too concerned about our reputation to take steps of faith when you ask us to. We need your wisdom to know how and when to be "fools for Christ"!

It is truly humbling that you choose to use us, as weak and foolish as we are, and we are in awe of the extravagance of your grace in providing our needs. Thank you!

Amen.

*Les handing over nursery in 2003
after building work completed.*

Chapter Fourteen

Lottery Funding

Dirty money or God's provision?

ONE OF THE BIG QUESTIONS THAT FACED US WAS WHETHER to apply for Lottery funding. Lottery funding was available for groups like our own who were reaching out to help and support the vulnerable and marginalised in society. However, to be able to apply, we would need to overturn a decision which prohibited Elim churches applying — a decision that had been taken at our Annual Conference some years before. There didn't seem to be the heart for a debate over this issue at the time as it was argued that the Lottery was wrong: it was gambling, and gambling has ruined many people's lives, so we Christians won't touch it. End of!

But in 2002, I felt that times were changing and maybe, just maybe, the members of the Conference would see things a little differently. Some of the older stalwarts of the movement had since retired, some new pastors and lay people were bringing in fresh ideas, and some were beginning to reimagine what church ministry might look like, especially in terms of its community involvement — the kind of schemes that could potentially be awarded such funding.

I spoke with our church leadership team to ascertain what they thought about receiving Lottery money for our projects in the future, and emphasised that should any one of them have a problem over this we would simply not apply for Lottery Funding, even if the Conference would allow us. Basically, each member of our local leadership team had the power of veto as we did not want to trample on any person's conscience or integrity. In love for our fellow leaders we would never ask them to do something if it was going against their consciences. Our love for each other was far more important than funding. We discussed it in depth, but no one had even the slightest of problems over applying to the

Lottery, so the next step was to raise this issue at Elim's Business Conference and attempt to change our constitution.

Some pastors are very political and have amazing ability to speak on technical and legal aspects of our Movement's constitution. Their speeches are often witty, powerful and even profound. I am not in the same league as any of them. In fact, the very thought of standing up at our Conference to speak before so many seasoned campaigners on a subject so controversial to them as Lottery Funding filled me with dread, but it needed to be done.

To present an item for the agenda of the Conference one needs a proposer, who was me, and a seconder, who was the Administrator of our Movement, Bruce Hunter. Bruce was trained as a lawyer and had amazing respect in our Movement. The term Administrator for his role didn't do it justice as he was a Senior Executive of our Movement, and a pastor. I was quite surprised that he kindly agreed to run with me on this proposal of allowing Elim churches to apply for Lottery Funding should they wish to.

The dreaded day came and as I walked to the front of the auditorium with many hundreds of our Movement's leaders present, my heart was virtually jumping out of my chest, as I was very junior and not very good at this sort of thing. Here is my speech on "Why we should be able to apply to the Lottery." You might passionately disagree with what I said, but I can live with that; at least, you will know where I was coming from. (For those who are interested, I include the full speech on why I believe it is acceptable to receive Lottery money. But if this doesn't "float your boat" then move on to the end of this speech.)

A few years ago, I, along with the vast majority of you, voted for a block on receiving Lottery money. I didn't need to think too hard about my decision, for, after all, I don't do the Lottery myself and I do not want to be perceived as endorsing gambling.

Looking back, I believe that my vote was a knee-jerk reaction and together as a Conference body we did not think through the implications of our decision. Forgive me for saying this, but I believe that we were a bit "gung-ho" and "tub thumping" in our condemnation of Lottery Funding. I also believe that we have scored a massive "own goal" in the decision we made.

Needless to say, upon reflection, and upon looking at some of the facts of Lottery funding, I have changed my mind on this issue. All I ask from you today is that you keep an open mind before you make your decision. As someone said, "Prejudice is a great timesaver, as it enables a person to give opinions without looking at the facts."

National Lottery funding is one of the government's main ways of supporting charitable and community projects. However, the responsibility for distributing proceeds from the Lottery doesn't rest with the Government, neither does it rest with the Lottery. It rests with 4 national arts councils, 4 national sports councils, UK Sport, the Heritage Fund, the Millennium Commission, the New Opportunities Fund, the Film Council and Awards for All. These independent bodies distribute funding in accordance with a framework of government policies.

Whether we like it or not, we cannot escape the reaches of the Lottery Fund. For example, the New Opportunities Fund (NOF) has given £750m for sport in schools; £44m to allow children to take part in adventure holidays; £213m on projects helping to reduce coronary heart disease and cancer; £200m on child care; £159m on community regeneration. If you have schoolteachers in your congregations, they will also tell you that a half of all secondary schools and a quarter of all primary schools have received NOF funding. In fact, our county council has received NOF funding for After Schools Care and is eager to fund an After Schools Scheme in our church. Presently, socially active churches that are touching the heart of their communities have their hands tied behind their backs. They are attempting to serve people in deep need. The government is saying, "Here is some money," and we are saying, "No, thank you!"

If we choose to refuse to receive Lottery funding out of conscience, that's fine; but if that is our chosen position, then perhaps out of integrity we need to go the whole way by not using the hospital that has received Lottery funding, or the school that has benefitted in this way, or that football club or gymnastics group that we send our children to on Saturday mornings. How many of us might have received free entry into that museum or art gallery, all because they have been funded by the Lottery?

I thank God that we live in a country where the government is willing to redirect 25p in the pound to charitable and community projects. This is something to be excited about and to celebrate, not something to bad-mouth and be suspicious of. Money is neither good nor evil; it is what we do with money that counts. We can use money for good or bad. There is no such thing as "dirty" money. We do not know where the money in our offering baskets comes from. It might be from gambling. It might be from prostitution. It might be from fiddling the tax man. Besides, I just wonder how many church leaders would refuse a tithe from a church member who has just won the Lottery. And whilst I have never bought a Lottery ticket, if we think that our church members don't do the Lottery, then we are detached from reality.

Please do not misunderstand what this proposal is all about — I'm not asking for all churches to apply to the Lottery. I am simply asking that those churches which are involved in community projects are not prevented from doing so, if they feel it is right. I want each church to have the freedom and opportunity to go this way if they believe that it is a door that God is opening to them. Besides, if you wish to apply for Lottery funding for a church building extension or for new chairs for your auditorium, or for 300 Bibles, you will be disappointed. The various Lottery-based funds are not for the so-called religious activity of churches, and churches that do nothing more than meet for Christian services will not be able to apply for funding anyway.

It is inevitable that there will be a number of speakers against this proposal. They will tell you essentially one of four things:

1. "By taking Lottery money, we are endorsing gambling." Do we endorse alcoholism by having a glass of wine? Do we endorse gluttony by eating three meals a day? Do we endorse child labour in third world sweatshops by buying clothes from

certain high street shops? This is money that the government is making available for those who desire to make a difference in their communities.

2. "We don't need the Lottery. The Lord will provide!" This sounds very spiritual! My argument is that the Lord has already provided. Why ask the Lord for other means of provision when the money is "there and waiting" for many of the types of projects our churches are planning or already running?

3. "We will ruin the testimony and witness of the church." I ask myself, who is most concerned about taking Lottery money? It is certainly not unbelievers. 75% of the country actually do the Lottery weekly and are happy with money going to charitable use. Your average Joe Bloggs doesn't think "hypocrite" should a church apply for and receive a Lottery Grant for help in feeding the homeless. He thinks, "Well done!" What's more, when average Joe Bloggs hears of petty rules that prevent churches from doing good, that is what turns his stomach. He would probably utter something about being "too heavenly minded for any earthly use". The average non-Christian would think of a church that turns down the offer of funding for a community project as embracing a quirky ideal!

4. "Gambling ruins people's lives" — which, sadly, it does occasionally. But for every one life that is ruined by gambling — which will happen whether we take lottery grants or not! — we can help and benefit the lives of scores, if not hundreds of people. Think of the good it will do. Think of the benefits for the church in the community and the gospel. Think of the lives you can touch!

My argument is not watertight. I am not writing a thesis for some external examiner. I am speaking to fellow brothers and sisters in the gospel. This is a heart thing. The resolution was passed in 1997 as a knee-jerk reaction. All I'm asking is that you will consider seriously, and in a considered way, the big picture.

I am willing to risk the label of endorsing gambling, if by doing so our Tamworth church might be able to touch the lives of needy people both practically and, maybe, eternally? It is a risk that I would be very willing to take. You might not be. That's OK. I will not despise you, but I pray that you would be magnanimous enough to allow me to make a choice according to my conscience. That's all I ask.

One last thought:

We thank God for the government's decision in allowing churches to benefit from the Gift Aid scheme. In fact, where would we be without it? It might be in a few years' time, we will be saying the same about the Community Fund and the Awards for All schemes and the New Opportunities Fund, aiding us to serve our communities in ways that we have not yet even conceived. One knee-jerk reaction was bad enough; please don't make another one today by voting against this proposal.

Looking back at my speech notes of 17 years ago, I am a little surprised at how direct I was back then, but then again, maybe I needed to be.

There was a polite ripple of applause, but I knew that I was on a hiding to nothing. There were a few speeches that followed mine, some for and some against the proposal. There were a number of others waiting in the wings to address this subject, but before that could happen, an older colleague had had enough of all this "nonsense" about Lottery money and called "to vote". When this happens, all speeches stop and the Conference body needs to decide on whether they are ready to vote on the main proposal or whether they wish to hear some more speeches. The decision was taken to not continue with the debate, but come to vote on my proposal, even before my seconder, Bruce, had had the opportunity to give his speech. The writing was on the wall. The chairman then asked for a show of hands of those who were in favour of my proposal to allow Elim churches to apply for Lottery funding. About 200 hands shot up, but I knew that was never going to be enough. Then the chairman asked for "those against" to raise their hands. The number against the proposal was overwhelming, but it appeared that the tide was beginning to turn, as five years earlier virtually no one had backed the proposal.

Many of you will be thinking that God's will was done and "thank goodness that the majority had the good sense to quash such an unholy proposal" and I am very happy for you to have your view on this, but I continue to believe this is one of those many grey areas where there is no right or wrong answer, merely personal preferences and arguments.

Speaking with Bruce following this disappointing result, and asking where we could go next, he suggested that there might be another way. He recommended that Tamworth Elim Church should consider setting up its own charitable company. We could have the church eldership team as directors or trustees of this charity, and they could make their own decision on whether to receive Lottery funding. And that is exactly what we did, not only to enable us to apply for Lottery funding but to allow us to move quickly "on the ground". Needing to refer back to our headquarters can be an unwieldy and tiresome process, so to have the ability to make decisions locally was hugely advantageous. The success of our community projects has been considerably enhanced by having our own local charitable company.

We set up the Manna House (Tamworth) Company in 2002. The name "Manna House" had already been used by our church for the coffee shop and centre adjacent to our church building for the previous six years, so it seemed the sensible thing to do to associate the charitable company with the good community name of the Manna House. All of our existing community projects and ministries that weren't directly related to church activities (coffee shop, bookshop, housing project, day nursery, counselling *etc.*) were brought under the banner of the Manna House charity, whilst the more typical church ministries remained under the church's management. In years following, when new projects commenced (charity clothes shop, elderly luncheon clubs, Foodbank and so forth) they became part of the charity. The church and charity are two separate legal and charitable entities, but in effect, both are led by the same people. So, during church leaders' meetings, there are two separate agendas and two sets of minutes, with occasional crossover in our discussion. Each year, we host an AGM which includes details of financial statements on both entities. Sometimes it feels a little schizophrenic, but having our own local charity has been enormously beneficial to us. No regrets!

Dear Lord,

As Christians, we sometimes use that age-old maxim, "In essentials 'unity', in non-essentials 'liberty', but in all things 'charity'", but we confess that it is often easier said than done. We so easily misunderstand what is essential and non-essential and subsequently forget to act charitably to our brothers and sisters. Lord, forgive us.

Help us recognise that your Church is wonderfully diverse — in ages, nationalities, ethnicities, colour of our skin, socio-economics, education, life-experiences and so much more. Keep us united amidst our diversity, and may we declare your praises through our love for one another.

Lord Jesus, you were revealed as One who was full of truth and grace, and our prayer is that we would be too.

Amen.

CHAPTER FIFTEEN

Our Day in Court

NEXT, WE NEEDED TO MOVE FORWARD WITH THE TENDER-
ing process by getting quotes from building companies for this colossal
four-stage building project. It wasn't only to be decided on cost but also
on experience and expertise of the building contractors, as they would
need to enlist a wide range of subcontractors and oversee the work. This
needed to be a fair and impartial process. It was, but I was personally
delighted that my friend Les, who had previously worked on our Manna
House project seven years earlier, came top, not only in price quoted for
the work, but also in leading the most experienced company. I knew that
Les would see this work, not merely as another job, but as God's work.

From January 2003 to March 2004 our church moved out of its
building and met on Sundays in a local high school. It was a great time.
Admittedly, those who needed to regularly set up sound equipment undoubtedly found the 15 months quite demanding, but it was much easier
moving our Sunday church congregation to another place than it would
have been for our day nursery. It was important for the nursery work to
continue as an income stream as much as anything else, but of paramount
importance was the safety of children and staff on what was essentially a
building site. This was achieved by moving the nursery around the
campus as far away as possible from where the building work was going
on, and by erecting large, temporary safety walls.

Phase one, which included a new kitchen and an extra office, was
completed within a couple of months. Phase two, a new church annexe,
was completed after five months. Phase three, our new day nursery on
two floors, was completed by month eleven, and the final phase of
extending the church building to more than double was finished by
month fifteen. We moved back in, much to the excitement of our church
family, on Tuesday 30th March 2004. I remember the sense of wonder-

ment in everyone. The problem was that we were now feeling dwarfed in this much larger building. At least we now had room to grow again.

Our celebration was tempered by some unanticipated VAT payment demands. VAT on buildings is a self-evaluation tax, with the responsibility of zero-rated certification coming from the organisation doing the building, which is then presented to the builder. This was done by our accountant on our behalf. The trouble was that Her Majesty's Revenue and Customs (HMRC) didn't agree with our decision and contested our zero-rating. This meant potentially an extra £100,000 on to our bill. Ouch!

The main area of dispute was whether our new day nursery was an annexe or an extension. I won't bore you with the details, but an extension can never be zero-rated, while an annexe can be if it fulfils various other criteria. To cut a long story short, we contested the decision of HMRC and took them to tribunal. They took our challenge very seriously indeed because if we won the case, then our victory would become case law and would cost the Exchequer ultimately lots of money.

In the red corner, HMRC naturally had their own team of legal experts and also employed a barrister to argue their case and dismantle ours. And in the blue corner, we had Martin, our church elder, and me! A few weeks before the case was to be heard in the Birmingham courts, I was sent the bundle — that is, all the documents that our opponents would be referring to in the hearing, which incidentally was diarised for three days at court. Any aspirations that I had for becoming the next Kavanagh QC — remember John Thaw's brilliance in the courtroom? — evaporated when I started reading four lever-arch files of case law appertaining to the case. There was a moment when I thought I had bitten off more than I could chew — understatement! All this legal stuff was well outside my comfort zone and I needed to be a fast learner as I was up against a barrister in about three weeks' time. Some people talk about their 15 minutes of fame; well, for me it was potentially three days of torture, but it had to be done. £100,000 was the prize.

I asked my fellow leaders to take care of preaching duties for the next few weeks while I concentrated on attempting to understand case law. Within days I realised that there were some aspects of our claim that we were never going to win, as case law had already decided the outcome. It would have been foolish to challenge this and a waste of court time. However, the annexe versus extension argument was very challengeable. So, for three weeks, my office was a mass of papers on every horizontal surface. Staff members acted like cornermen, or seconds, in the boxing ring assisting their man to fight another round. I was fed lots of caffeine and encouragement: "You can do it, Steve. You are our champion!" No, they didn't actually say those words, but I felt the weight of expectation and responsibility on my shoulders.

The dreaded day had come (6th June 2005) and I had never been so nervous in my life. I knew that I couldn't blag my way out of this. I reckon that I am a person with average intelligence, but I was not going to be any match for a trained barrister on his home turf. We arrived at the courts and had a preliminary meeting with the other side's legal team. They were willing to concede on a couple of points and we were also willing to concede on some other areas where case law favoured them.

The one point they wanted to challenge was our new nursery, which was linked to our main church auditorium. Was it an extension, as they claimed, or an annexe and potentially zero-rated, as we argued? Their barrister was a very polite younger man in a pinstripe suit. I replaced my usual open neck shirt and Levi's for a jacket and tie, which was probably for the best. In fact, the barrister couldn't have been any more helpful than he was. He probably thought it would be a simple open and shut case, an easy day at the office for him, but as the tribunal got underway, he got crankier and crankier. I was the main spokesperson, and Martin, who sat on my right, acted as my solicitor, feeding me the various legal papers and occasionally whispering advice.

At the beginning of the afternoon session, I needed to change hats from being the presenter of our case to being cross-examined by the opposing barrister, something that I was not looking forward to. However, my copious reading of case law over the previous three weeks helped me anticipate where his line of questioning was headed, and to be tighter and more technical in my language than I might have been otherwise.

The real "killer" for me was when the judge asked me to present my concluding argument. I was initially floored by this and asked his permission to have some time to gather my thoughts. He kindly agreed and gave me 30 minutes to do so, but by this time my brain had frazzled and I found it very demanding to collect my thoughts, let alone convincingly argue my barrister friend under the table. I did my best, which is all I could do, and felt emotionally empty after such a tough day. They never told me about my needing to be an amateur barrister when I was a theology student at Elim Bible College in the 1980s.

We waited for several weeks before the judgment. Sadly, we lost, but upon careful scrutiny of the judgement notice, I became aware that the judge had based his decision on a crucial misunderstanding of the material facts. I believed that if he had not made such a mistake, he would not have judged in favour of our opponents. I wrote to both HMRC and to the judge, who later wrote back to me, offering words of regret with regards to his factual errors, but he also communicated his inability to correct them. I appreciated his honesty, but it did not help a small local charity whose purpose was to serve and support the most vulnerable people in our community.

But how could this error be corrected? Whilst we didn't have the money to pour into legal representation, which was the reason why I needed to represent us in the first place, we did need a barrister to cast his eyes over the judgment. He too agreed that there had been mistakes made but encouraged us to count our losses and not take this into a higher court.

A couple of months passed with post-tribunal skirmishes over the mistakes made at tribunal, exploring if there was another way forward for us to appeal the decision. We bit the bullet and wrote to HMRC requesting advice on how to pay the VAT money we owed. They didn't reply, at least not quickly, and since I wasn't in a rush to pay it, I just sat tight and allowed them to respond when they were good and ready. After a couple of months, they did reply with a bland, "I apologise for the delay in responding … I have forwarded a copy of your letter [to another section]". I wrote twice more in coming months to find out how we might pay the VAT that we owed HMRC. I finally received a letter, dated 18th September 2006 (more than 15 months after the tribunal), which again apologised for the long delay in responding, which to be honest didn't bother me at all. The letter restated that we were responsible for paying VAT, but included a certain caveat that made my heart leap inside my chest. I quote, "This is subject to no more than three years having elapsed since the end of the accounting period in which the original supply took place. If you or your supplier(s) require any further information concerning this point, please contact the National Advice Service on…"

I sensed that HMRC was throwing us a lifeline. Did this mean that all the VAT that should have been paid more than three years earlier was no longer payable? That is what the letter seemed to suggest. Further queries over several months were made with the National Advice Service, without a clear response. The result was that more than three years had elapsed, writing off all VAT payments on our buildings as they fell outside the relevant accounting period. I would not have known about this had they not informed me. So, we might have technically lost the tribunal, but I could live with that, given that we were released from the VAT payments that would have crippled us financially. Surely when circumstances like this bring us to our knees, it is never a bad thing! It was just one more example of God's sovereign and providential dealings with weak, feeble people trying to serve his purpose in his world.

Father God,

Thank you that you supply our needs, occasionally in ways which surprise us. You are amazing! You not only supply our needs materially, but you also supply us with the ability to serve you in areas for which we are not trained, and sometimes beyond our life experiences — but then again, you choose to use the foolish things and the weak things of this world to confound the so-called wise and strong, and in doing so you get all the glory. We thank you that you laugh at impossibilities. Help us to expect great things from you and attempt great things for you, for your honour and praise.

Amen.

*The new Elim Church building following the massive
four-phase extension in 2003-2004, which included a
64-place day nursery, annexe, industrial kitchen, and a
worship space more than doubling capacity.*

Chapter Sixteen

New Buildings, New Opportunities

A ministry to the elderly

AS LOVELY AS OUR NEW BUILDINGS WERE, COMPLETE WITH new chairs, curtains, carpets, where everything was freshly painted and functioning, we still spoke of our church auditorium as a sheep-shed for sheep. This was not meant to be impolite about our church worship space or, worse still, being disrespectful to God, but it was a gentle reminder that we do not worship a building. We thank God for our buildings which are a wonderful resource, and a great tool for us to serve the purposes of God, but we were not going to be so precious about bricks and mortar and materials that we would prohibit their use for anything other than Sunday worship. We keep well away from calling the auditorium a "sanctuary" (derived from the Latin *sanctus,* meaning "holy") for it is the people who make the room holy and not the other way around. The building is not the church, but a place where the church meets. Practically, the benefit of having individual, stackable chairs, rather than the old wooden pews of some traditional churches, means that we can use this resource for a wide range of church ministries and outreaches.

As with the Manna House centre eight years earlier, our new church buildings would provide us with an amazing resource for mission. For a few years, there had been a handful of mainly older people who had been chomping at the bit to launch a luncheon club to reach out to the elderly in our community with the love of Christ. Now that the nursery had its own space, the new church auditorium and annexe was available, and enabled us to move forward with our vision. The new industrial kitchen also meant that we could provide excellent meals for large numbers of people.

In June 2004, we commenced our very first Prime Time, a luncheon club for over 65s, mainly aimed at those who were socially isolated due to illness or immobility rather than those of the same age who were fit and healthy. Ken, who also helped us place international missions on our church agenda as our missions secretary, led this new "mission" amongst the elderly. Prime Time started with a great number of enthusiastic volunteers — cooking, using their cars to transport the elderly, serving meals, washing dishes and, most importantly, spending quality time with many people who lived on their own with little or no social interaction. From the very first day there was such an amazing feel-good factor. The Wednesday group became so popular that it grew to a maximum of 40 within a couple of months and we needed to expand to a second day. The Thursday group was launched in January 2005 and was again full within a few months. This placed a significant strain on the volunteer helpers and we knew that we could not sustain this level of activity in the long term, so we decided to apply for external grant funding to provide this fledgling ministry with a salaried co-ordinator and chef. This would take the strain off the volunteers who needed to organise the Prime Time luncheon club and cook for 80+ people each week.

Ken did well in taking the lead in the early days, but this could never be a long-term option for someone who was himself well into his retirement years. We got funding from the Lottery and employed a lady named Diane. Diane was an able lay leader at her Anglican church and took full leadership responsibilities during a long interregnum. She was also as good a stand-up comic as you would see anywhere, and an ideal person to help shape what was to become an award-winning social and luncheon club for the elderly at our church.

Our church mission statement is "Reaching Tamworth with the life-transforming love of Christ" and over the years, Prime Time has most certainly fulfilled that mission. We have never abused our privileged position by Bible-bashing people into submission, but we have sought to share the love of Christ with others and build community through our care and concern, which has often created the environment where people quite naturally ask us about our Christian faith. Since its inception, many, many lives have been enhanced and enriched — both attendees and volunteer helpers — and a good number have come to faith. Prime Time has brought purpose and joy to hundreds of local people.

Over the years, deep friendships have been formed with some of our members choosing to go on holidays with each another or in small groups, and many speak on the phone to each other daily. There have been friendships reunited when former school-friends found themselves sitting at the same table, having lost contact for 60 or 70 years. People like Ada, who attended until her late 90s, would tell us virtually every week how important Prime Time was to her, and that she would not meet another living soul until she was picked up again for Prime Time the following week, since her family had moved away from Tamworth. There were many like Ada, and there are many like her in your community too.

There have been two engagements — Richard and Eve, and Ken and Audrey — though, sadly, neither engagement led to marriage as both ladies died before they could "tie the knot". Richard and Eve were childhood sweethearts who parted and then got married to others. Following the passing of their spouses they found each other again through Prime Time. One day as Richard was musing over his love life, he laughed and said that he may be a man in his 80s, but in his mind he was still a young man with the same feelings and desires. He just couldn't do much about them anymore! The emotional difficulty in working with people of the third-age is that there are regular funerals, an empty seat at the table and sadness, though there is also an amazing resilience in those who experienced wartime Britain. In the last 14 years, Prime Time has welcomed about 400 people to its Wednesday and Thursday luncheons, with the majority of that number having now passed away.

Prime Time has also provided a lifeline to volunteer helpers like Cilla (not her real name) who had previously attempted suicide by taking an overdose. She often spoke of the group saving her life and providing her with a purpose and reason to live. She was a valued part of the team for a number of years before her delicate mental state got the better of her and she was taken into care.

Fun and laughter have been essential elements in Prime Time's success, and it is so wonderful to witnesses some people in their 80s and 90s dancing to tunes of yesteryear on our musical "specials" — dare I say it? — in the sanctuary! For many years, the volunteer helpers put on a Christmas Special, often a pantomime, much to the delight and merriment of the elderly. I regularly got roped into playing some part, whether it was Batman, Tom Jones (complete with head and chest wigs), a puppet on a string or the panto dame — often the latter! These times were a mixture of slapstick and silliness, but they brought such joy to our audience.

Each year, Diane organised a holiday for the group and went to exotic places like Weston-Super-Mare, Hayling Island, Isle of White and Great Yarmouth. One great memory was when a number of the group, most in their 80s and 90s, decided to have a hot air balloon ride. Daredevils! Another unforgettable moment was when Iris, not a small lady, fell off the coastal path on her mobility scooter. It was a small mercy that she didn't fall on to the rocks, but rather into a bush of brambles. Paramedics were called, but they couldn't help her due to her size and the upturned mobility scooter balancing precariously in the brambles. Since the air ambulance was on another job, the coastal rescue helicopter was commissioned and saved the day. She was later released from hospital with cuts and bruises, but no lasting damage. Happy memories!?

Many of our older friends were brought up in an age when children were sent to Sunday School, often to provide their parents with an hour's rest. Some of them had been regular church attenders whose faith had lapsed. Surprisingly few regarded themselves as atheists, militant or passive. The majority of them had no objection to grace being said before meals, or for a short religious service to be held following lunch at certain times during the year, which would include Christmas, Easter and Harvest. There were some, like Freda, who didn't object to being a part of a Christian club as long as no-one got too close to her tolerance levels. When the subject of Christianity was raised in private conversation, she always did her best to change the subject, and would often say that God would have nothing to do with her since he knew how bad she had been. Her reaction appeared to be a suppressed guilt stemming from her early Catholicism and the harsh treatment she received by those who taught her. Martin was a regular visitor to her home when Freda became too ill to attend Prime Time, and often encouraged her by saying that even though God knows everything about her, he loves her just the same. However, when he asked permission to pray for her, she would always decline. In the final year of her life, Freda became very ill and eventually was bed-bound, making it necessary for her to be moved into nursing care. Initially, she became fiercely angry at this and often refused visits, but as she grew frailer, she allowed some of the Prime Time team to visit her at the nursing home. One day, Martin sat beside her, praying quietly under his breath. She awoke and turned her eyes in his direction.

"Hello, Freda, it's Martin," he said.

She held out her slender and almost translucent hand for him to hold.

"May I pray with you?" he asked, and to his genuine surprise she quietly responded, "Yes, please."

Martin prayed that she would know God's grace, and that his never-failing love would comfort her and take her home to be with him. He asked God to give her peace and strength and that she would not be afraid, but instead to know the presence of God with her. She responded with a quiet "thank you" and the slightest smile. That was Martin's last visit, as she passed away some 48 hours later.

One of the great delights of Prime Time has been the way in which so many older people, both participants and volunteer helpers, have found a true faith in Jesus. Some found faith through being invited to join a special Prime Time Bible study group on a Tuesday afternoon, others through a monthly Sunday afternoon service and buffet, still others were invited to take part in an Alpha Course. The sheer joy and privilege of baptising people in their 70s and 80s and hearing them sharing their testimonies of God's grace has been incredibly inspiring.

There are many inspirational stories of transformed lives, but one deserves further comment: Richard. Richard was different in so many ways. He was a smartly dressed 80-year-old, always in shirt, tie, waistcoat and tweed jacket. This alone caused him to stand out amongst his contemporaries whose dress was usually far more casual. Richard had thinning grey hair swept back rather elegantly and a well-manicured grey moustache. Within minutes of meeting Richard, you would think, "What a delightful gentleman," with the emphasis on *gentle*. His face lit up with a beaming smile and he had a twinkle in his eyes. He always showed interest in others and was as articulate in speech as he was elegant in dress. When you spoke with Richard, you always came away feeling inspired.

Richard was house-bound and was introduced to Prime Time through his carer, who suggested that he could do with a regular outing and the opportunity to meet some new people. He jumped at the chance and, by his own testimony, was delighted to meet "some pretty wonderful people". Richard was intelligent and inquisitive and often asked searching questions about matters of faith. He had never considered it seriously, but conversations at Prime Time caused him to ponder the existence of God.

Richard was a man who wrote out his thoughts on paper in wonderful copperplate handwriting. In one such journal, he entitled the first page, "My search for God." In his own inimitable way, not too unlike C. S. Lewis, he agreed with the concept of God, for when one observes the magnificence and wonder of creation, there must surely be a Designer. However, for Richard, the Resurrection of Christ initially proved a stumbling block. After giving his position some serious thought, he realised that he wasn't being especially logical, for if there was a God, then surely God by definition could do anything he wanted to do, including raising Christ from the dead.

In a later video testimony,[14] Richard told of an incident that occurred that brought his search for God to an end. He relates of a time when he sat up in bed in the early hours of one Sunday morning, trying to write down his thoughts. He'd been complaining to God about his predicament of having a family that he'd never met. He mused that God seems to be too preoccupied with the really consequential things in the world, but not the small and insignificant things, like the problems he had. He protested to God that he had reached a mature age, was still grieving for his wife, and was generally bemoaning his fate. He felt quite fed up as he attempted to clear his thoughts. Then an idea came to him that he should purchase a writing desk so that he could sit down in comfort and collate his reflections.

Later that morning, a friend called at his house and invited him to go out for the day. Richard asked if they could go to an antiques furniture shop that he had heard about. The first thing that Richard saw as he entered the shop was a writing desk with an attractive green top. Richard purchased the desk and went out to lunch with his friend. After lunch, the desk was carried out to their vehicle by the proprietor and an elderly gentleman with white hair.

The proprietor said, "By the way Richard, this person" — gesturing to the other man — "has the same surname as you." Richard got out of the car and asked him where he lived. "Weddington," he said.

"Oh, I used to live there when I was a child, with my father," said Richard.

"My grandfather used to live there," responded the other gentleman.

"What was his name?" asked Richard.

---

[14] To view Richard sharing his story:
go to *www.tamworth-elim.org.uk*; scroll down until you come across the 'media and sermons' button; click, then scroll down to the series 'Big Questions'; click 'Personal story in memory of Richard Latham.'
I'll guarantee that you will love this video!

"James," came the reply.

"What was your father's name?" asked Richard.

"That was James too. I also had a brother named James, but he got captured at Dunkirk."

On hearing this, the hair on the back of Richard's neck started prickling. He stood up close to this stranger, looked him in the eye, and said, "Yes, I know, and he was force-marched across Poland with only a bag of sugar to sustain him."

The other man looked at Richard with astonishment and said, "Good heavens, how did you know that?"

Richard replied, "Because I am your brother. The one you've never met!"

Richard says that they embraced long and hard, and he had a peculiar sensation come over him as he realised that only a few hours prior he had been complaining to God about having a family he'd never met, and lo and behold, it had come about within a matter of a few hours!

Richard concluded, "So now the God of my imagination has disappeared and the real God has come into my heart. So, from then on, I was 100% convinced. As I say, my search for God has ended, but I shall still be asking questions — it's only human I suppose."

Richard has since passed on, but left us with such wonderful memories as have so many of our Prime Time friends. We can truly say that our lives have been enriched in so many ways by them.

Lord,

Thank you for the gift of friendship. We treasure memories of sharing special moments, fun and laughter, joyous conversation or convivial debate. Sometimes, we've needed a shoulder to cry on or some good advice and have been grateful for the listening ear of a friend.

We pray for people in our communities who are isolated. Help us to reach out to them, Lord, and find ways to ease their burden of loneliness. May they find comfort in knowing you — the God who controls the universe, yet is attentive to our needs, even those seemingly inconsequential concerns that niggle us.

Thank you that in you we find a friend who sticks closer than a brother.

Amen.

CHAPTER SEVENTEEN

The Tough Years (1)

The storm clouds are gathering

WHILST IT WAS ENCOURAGING TO SEE THE CHURCH CON-gregation grow slowly but surely, it was even more spiritually satisfying to see the wider impact of the church in the community. Church surely shouldn't be measured by the number of bottoms on seats on a Sunday morning service, but by the impact a church is making for God's kingdom every day of the week. We were seeking to be "Christ" to everyone we met. In truth, there were hundreds of people who spoke of Elim Church as being their church, even though the vast majority did not attend our Sunday services. We have often said that *belonging* comes before *believing*, which is the antithesis of many churches. I remember a time when there was an emphasis on believing before belonging — that is, that people could only truly belong once they had accepted the foundational truths of their church, and signed up to become fully-fledged members. At Tamworth Elim, we quite deliberately and unashamedly focus our efforts on creating community and helping people to belong, which often encourages them towards a place of believing and trusting Christ.

On the journey, we have experienced a number of challenges and difficulties, but nothing like those that were about to befall us. We had experienced some heady days in my first twelve years at Tamworth and were making a significant impact on our community, but the clouds were growing darker in a range of ways.

In late autumn of 2004, Julie detected a lump on her breast which sent me into a tailspin of concern and anxiety. She made an appointment with our doctor who sent her for a hospital appointment and biopsy. The result of the biopsy was that the tumour was pre-cancerous, but they couldn't be entirely sure until they had removed it. For the first time in our married lives, I was confronted by the possibility of serious illness and ultimately death. Although Julie seemed to be taking her condition very much in her stride, my mind was working overtime and I became very frightened at the possibility of her becoming seriously ill. The whole process from the time of the discovery of the tumour to the time it was extracted and then checked for cancer cells was interminable. I could not think of anything else during these few weeks. I am normally so resilient, but this was an Achilles' heel to me. I was thankful to God that when the results came back, they showed that there were no cancer cells present, but Julie required regular check-ups for the next few years.

Around this time, a young lady "R" telephoned the Manna House centre on the afternoon of 2nd November 2004, stating that she was on the verge of committing suicide. She asked if a minister could ring her back immediately. As soon as I got the message, I returned her call. She claimed that she was about to leave a satanist group and was very, very frightened at what her former associates would do to her. I agreed to meet with her, along with my associate pastor, Paul, at 5.30pm. In agreeing to meet with her, we had no real idea of what the next four weeks would hold. "R" got out of her taxi, barely able to walk. I helped her to the church, sat her down and offered refreshments. She was in a terrible state and was being controlled by demonic forces which were responsible for a range of physical behaviours: changing of facial features; fluttering of eyelids; only the whites of her eyes being visible; panic; agitation; falling forwards on to her face; spitting; blaspheming; writhing on her back, snake-like; snarling through gritted teeth. Many evil spirits were cast out in the course of the evening. I had never experienced such an extreme case of demonization in my ministry. Following this "episode", which I admit caught me a little flat-footed, I thereafter always made sure that we had at least one lady ministering with us in this kind of deliverance ministry as a protection against any fallacious allegations that might have been targeted at us. Many of the evil spirits took over "R's" voice, with a variety of accents and voices, and with the demons naming themselves: Lucifer; Fear; Death; Antichrist; Hate; Satan (named after his master!); Orgy; False Religion; Church of Jesus Christ of Latter Day Saints (I kid you not!); Confusion; Darkness; Deception; and many, many others. Some demons came out in clusters. For example, False Religion, Latter Day Saints, Deception and Confusion were all linked.

During this time, I was sickened to hear of some of the nauseating practices of those involved in satanic rituals. I have no intention of repeating them for two reasons. Firstly, I have no desire to fill my readers' minds with the sheer evil of what I learned from "R" and her insights into satanism. Secondly, if I did choose to share what I learned of in a four-week period in November 2004, most people would not believe me anyway. It all would sound too far-fetched and unbelievable. I remember going home and explaining to Julie what I witnessed. She responded by making me promise not to tell anyone because "people will think you've lost the plot".

I was interested to learn from "R" that Satanists didn't mind if she or anyone else involved in satanic practices joined another religion, as long as it wasn't Christianity. There was also a certain fear when she came in close proximity to a Bible. One morning she entered our church building when the congregation was singing its praises to Jesus:

> *Jesus shall take the highest honour,*
> *Jesus shall take the highest praise.*
> *Let all earth join heaven in exalting*
> *The Name which is above all other names.*
> *Let's bow the knee in humble adoration*
> *For at His name every knee must bow.*
> *Let every tongue confess He is Christ, God's only Son;*
> *Sovereign Lord, we give You glory now,*
> *For all honour and blessing and power*
> *Belongs to You, belongs to You;*
> *All honour and blessing and power*
> *Belongs to You, belongs to You,*
> *Lord Jesus Christ, Son of the living God.*

God's presence was so manifest that she simply collapsed in the doorway. The spirits that controlled her could not cope with the majesty and splendour of Jesus being proclaimed by worshipping people.

It didn't take long for our church family to start asking questions about this strange young woman. Some were deeply concerned for their safety and the safety of their families, others were concerned over why "R" wasn't being delivered by Christ, so I needed to write an Open Letter to our church. I was patently aware of the subtlety of this attack and the possibility of it dividing our members, so I encouraged those with questions or concerns to speak with me or another member of our church leadership team rather than voice their disquiet to others in the church, with the potential of generating division and further distraction.

I openly shared with the church family that despite this area of ministry being relatively new to us, our church leadership was not immature or naïve. We were very aware that we were engaged in a spiritual battle, not against flesh and blood but against demonic forces and the schemes of Satan, and requested the church to pray for this young lady to be released from the demonic forces and for the protection of our church.

I remember one demon that named itself Antichrist being cast out. There was a blood-curdling scream from "R" and all the fuses tripped in the Manna House centre. In all, there were literally hundreds of demons cast out. Each time we thought we were making a spiritual breakthrough, we were nearly always disappointed. She often took two steps forward and three backwards, but why was that? We were deeply concerned over her apparent desire to be set free — and for a short while she was in a better place — but she was actually getting worse overall. It took us a couple of weeks to realise that things were not as they appeared on the surface.

I was reminded of what Jesus taught in Luke 11:24-26: "When an impure spirit comes out of a person, it goes through arid places seeking rest and does not find it. Then it says, 'I will return to the house I left.' When it arrives, it finds the house swept clean and put in order. Then it goes and takes seven other spirits more wicked than itself, and they go in and live there. And the final condition of that person is worse than the first." That is what appeared to be happening with "R". She kept disappearing for a couple of days at a time, always coming back with some new story of her whereabouts and how she escaped from the clutches of her satanic comrades, but I was far from convinced. Each time, I could see that something in her had changed; a new power, a darkness and greater resistance to Jesus.

The only thing that we could put this down to was that she was on some kind of satanic mission to disrupt our church. If that was the case, it was working! Some people were praying more fervently than ever before, but many others were frightened and deeply concerned about their leaders. For the first three weeks of this girl being around, all we seemed to do was focus on delivering her from demonic forces. She would turn up in our coffee shop and start manifesting demonic behaviour, so it was hard to ignore her.

I have often asked the Lord for the "ability to distinguish between spirits" (see 1 Cor. 12:10) at times when someone who is hearing destructive voices asks for prayer or counselling. I am not a Pentecostal believer who thinks that every "voice" is of the devil and needs to be cast out. In ministry, I have become aware of other reasons for such voices, like Multiple Personality Disorder or Dissociative Identity Disorder (DID). Disassociation is a defence mechanism and many with DID have had a traumatic event in childhood, such as physical, sexual or emotional abuse, which causes their personality to fragment into other identities — each with their own names, voices, personal histories and mannerisms, even handwriting. Switching off from reality is a normal defence mechanism that can help a person cope through a time of unbelievable trauma such as war, kidnapping or indeed Satanic Ritual Abuse (SRA).[15]

I personally know someone whose disassociation came through SRA, and the unspeakable evils that she suffered at the hands of her satanist parents and their friends. Now a Christian, she has many "personalities" whom she refers to as "The Gang", and has learned to live a purposeful life despite the fragmentation of her personality. To many well-meaning pastors, her condition might understandably sound demonic rather than psychological.

It is always troublesome to me when a pastor or church leader fails to recognise psychological factors, and also when a psychiatrist or psychologist fails to recognise spiritual factors. If the cause is psychological then the answer is found in psychology, and no amount of claiming victory in Jesus or attempting to cast out demons will help the person. The trauma of attempted exorcism might even be seriously detrimental. Conversely, if the cause is spiritual and demonic, then no amount of attempting to integrate personalities on a psychiatrist's couch will be successful. Demonic spirits simply need to be cast out!

Coming back to "R": I'm unsure whether there were any psychological factors or not. I'm not a psychologist. But given what she conveyed to me about her experiences, I would not be surprised if she experienced some disassociation of personalities. The one thing I do know with certainty, there was significant demonic activity and "R" appeared to be on some kind of satanic mission.

I knew that this could not carry on any longer as the leadership of our church was being worn down and the pastors were distracted from our mission. So, I did some detective work with some well-placed

---

[15] For a fascinating insight into this condition, Carolyn Bramhall, *Am I a Good Girl?* Oxford, Monarch Books, 2005.

contacts, which took me initially to Cambridge where "R" had hounded one church, even stalking the pastor when he and his family were away on holiday. Her presence had devastated the work and ministry there. The pastor asked me how long she had been with us. I told him that it was less than a month, to which he responded, "Well done!" as she had disrupted his church for a year, and he knew of another church that had suffered her disruptive presence for three years.

Given all the background information I'd gleaned, I was now surer than ever that "R" was not genuinely seeking to be released from her enslavement but was on some kind of mission. One piece of information she passed to me was that the police were looking for her as she had previously jumped bail. As much as I wanted to give her one more chance, because that is the way that I am wired, I knew that I needed to play hardball with her and informed her that should I see her around our premises ever again, I would immediately call the police. I also informed all 550 or so Elim churches of her activities. The following week, a pastor friend of mine telephoned from Edinburgh, Scotland, to thank me for my email as she had turned up at his church. Incredibly sad story!

Since that awful month I have met others, from time to time, who had opened their lives to the occult and were spiritually enslaved through demonic forces, although nothing to the extent of "R". It isn't something I see every week — thank the Lord — but I doubt whether any pastor will serve out his or her entire ministry without coming face to face with some of this stuff. These days, I am less inclined to think that this battle is a power struggle, but a truth struggle. It is the truth that shall set a person free. Demons are very tiresome and not very creative. When you've encountered one, you will meet much the same tactics with all the others: the cursing, blaspheming, spitting, snarling, the insults and aggression, the power talk: "You think you are so strong, but you are not! You think you are a man of God; you're not. I am more powerful than you," *etc.* It's akin to Key Stage 1 playground banter: "My dad's stronger than your dad!"

If you have never encountered this kind of enslavement before, it might sound very spectacular and spiritually cutting edge, but to be honest, I'd rather be cleaning the drains. These days, I try not to converse with the evil spirit; I just speak to the person who is demonised. I encourage them to take authority over their own lives, repent and confess those areas where they permitted dark forces to enter, and acknowledge the Lordship of Christ, thus not giving permission or any "right" for the spirit to possess the person any longer. In my experience, when a person does this they often struggle to speak. Some have a severe choking sensation and are unable to breathe, which can be very disturbing to an onlooker. At this point I have commanded spirits to release the person, so that she/he can take control over her/his own destiny. I could say so much more about this stuff, but I have probably said more than enough already! It was C. S. Lewis who once wrote, "There are two equal and opposite errors into which our race can fall about the devils. One is to disbelieve in their existence. The other is to believe, and to feel an excessive and unhealthy interest in them. They themselves are equally pleased by both errors and hail a materialist or a magician with the same delight."[16] I certainly do not wish to fall foul of Lewis's excellent advice by writing any more on this subject. Let's move on.

Dear Lord,

Our desire is always to worship you in spirit and truth. We know that there is nothing and no-one greater or more praiseworthy than you. We rest in our conviction that "neither death nor life, neither angels nor demons, neither the present nor the future, nor any powers, neither height nor depth, nor anything else in all creation, will be able to separate us from the love of God that is in Christ Jesus our Lord."

Guard our hearts and minds from an unhealthy interest in any form of evil, and grant us wisdom to help those who are trapped in its clutches. We are mindful that "our struggles are not against flesh and blood, but against the powers of this dark world and against the spiritual forces of evil in the heavenly realms". We also know that our Lord Jesus has won the victory over sin and death and darkness! Hallelujah!

Amen.

---

[16] C. S. Lewis, *The Screwtape Letters,* New York, Harpers Collins, 1996, xi.

CHAPTER EIGHTEEN

The Tough Years (2)

How much more, Lord?

WE WERE NOT THROUGH THE STORM JUST YET. THERE WERE hurricane winds and hailstones the size of golf balls awaiting us. At the time of Julie's medical concerns, I received a letter from the General Superintendent of Elim who wrote on 14th January 2005, on behalf of the National Leadership Team, requesting that I give account of my theological understanding on the work of the Holy Spirit, as it was felt that I might have embraced some views which were unorthodox and outside the foundational tenets of our Movement's beliefs. I was invited to meet with a member of the National Leadership Team and the principal of the Theological College. I could have really done without this uninvited burden just at that moment. The perfect storm was brewing!

Unashamedly, I am a Pentecostal Christian. I believe in the present work of the Holy Spirit in the world today. I believe in the gifts of the Spirit. I believe in tongues and prophecy. I personally speak in tongues and thank God for this gift of a prayer language, but I have never been a "classical" Pentecostal — one who believes that Christian initiation is in two distinct stages: conversion and baptism in the Holy Spirit, which, I believe, can often create a first and second class Christian mentality.

I believe that one receives the Holy Spirit at conversion, and it is from the gift of the Spirit that all spiritual gifts flow. One doesn't require a subsequent "baptism in the Holy Spirit" as some kind of second-stage distinctive "blessing", though, of course, the life in the Spirit will undoubtedly include many experiences that could be referred to as "fillings" of the Spirit. My personal view largely follows that of Professors Gordon Fee, Max Turner and Wayne Grudem, among others.

I would be the first to recognise that in a Movement like Elim, mine would be the minority view. Even so, I believed that our Movement's foundational beliefs were wide enough to embrace my nuanced view of the Spirit's work. I believed passionately in the Spirit's work and the gifts of the Spirit for today but could not agree that there was some distinct and subsequent baptism in the Holy Spirit. Please don't bother writing to me to correct my theology by quoting some "classical" theologian, because I have probably read those books too!

As far as I was concerned, my views were what they had always been, but there was a request, for whatever reason, that I should now be questioned over them, with the consequence of my needing to stand down from office if it was judged that I had crossed this theological line. This was unasked for and painful to me. To be honest, I didn't see it coming and was surprised by the suddenness of this onslaught.

It felt as though I were wading through treacle at this time, for I was worried about Julie's health, we had just experienced a month from "hell" (excuse the pun) with "R", and now I was being challenged over my beliefs by the leaders of my Movement with the possibility of losing my ministerial credential and vocation. Over the weeks that passed, there were various letters sent to and from me, and to and from our church eldership to the General Superintendent and National Leadership Team. With all this going on it was exceptionally difficult to concentrate my thoughts on just being a pastor. I was so, so grateful for the amazing support from my eldership team at Tamworth during this torrid time.

In due course, I decided to meet with the two leaders as requested, much against the advice of my eldership team who were dismayed over the manner of this confrontation. Colin and William came from London and Nantwich to meet with me. It was a pleasant conversation and we were able to agree on many things, but differed on this one issue of a baptism in the Holy Spirit being subsequent to conversion. I expected little else.

I had now fulfilled all that was requested of me by my leaders. I had met with my colleagues, explained in great detail what I believed, and now it was over to them to report back to the National Leadership Team. I would have been disappointed and deeply saddened if my days with Elim were coming to a close, but that decision was out of my hands.

On 24th May 2005, I received a letter from the General Superintendent, confirming that I could retain my ministerial credential. The decision was made, and I was deemed theologically sound "enough" to remain in the fold, but the whole process, five months in all, was heavy-handed and to my mind unnecessary. In writing about this incident, please do not think that I am holding on to any unforgiveness, I'm not — if indeed there was anything to forgive — but as much as I respect my leaders in Elim, in hindsight this whole process was, in my view, clumsy, a sledgehammer to crack a nut, if you will! And I was the nut! No comments please.

What I have written over the last few pages is just a taste of what life was to become in the next few years. There were situations that took me to the limits of my endurance and grace. In fact, if you wrap all the items that I've already mentioned together, multiply them by ten, you will not be anywhere close to the pain and disruption that we were about to encounter as a church. We thank God for his grace, in that he removes our transgressions and sins from us, as far as the east from the west. He offers us a clean slate and a new start. The apostle Paul writes, "There is no condemnation in Christ" (Rom. 8:1) and tells us that if anyone is in Christ, he is a new creation and that the old has gone and everything becomes new (2 Cor. 5:17). I believe that passionately, and my guess is that if you've got this far through this book, you believe it too! This spiritual regeneration is at the heart of the Christian life, but often the consequences of our past sins remain with us. For example, a murderer might find forgiveness with God, but the victim is still dead and families are still devastated, and when the police apprehend the murderer, he will get a jail sentence. He couldn't just say to the police, "God has forgiven me so everything is fine." Forgiveness is real but the consequences of our sins can often catch up with us, sometimes many decades later.

Whilst I have no desire to speak of specific issues that even today remain painful to talk about, for a period of about two years I needed to deal with recriminations associated with our church that stemmed back to a time long before I arrived on the scene in 1992. This time was painful for all those wounded by past events, and for the whole church community. Having said that, the church family was astonishing in its gracious and compassionate reaction to the desperate pain that so many were experiencing. As excruciating as this time was for everyone, the amazing church family at Elim came up trumps, and forgiveness and mercy flowed. In times of utter desperation and darkness, Christ's light and comfort are most tangibly felt.

During this time, I regularly found as much as half my week was taken up dealing with the fall-out and brokenness that bygone sin had caused. As I say, the church family were precious and supportive, but there were others, both in Tamworth and much further afield, who seemed to revel in busybodying. I have often referred to their "contribution" as the righteous indignation of the uninvolved! Gossip, innuendo and slander at this time were directed at our church, and often at me personally. It was exhausting. Thankfully, through the toughest days we can know the presence of Christ, not forgetting that in our weakness, he is strong. My weakness was palpable but so was his strength.

I'm not sure what this is like to read, but it isn't especially easy to write. So, you might ask, why bother? I want to bother simply because it is so important to share the whole story, not just the spectacular bits when God really moved amongst us or when prayers were answered. There were awful days; days when I could hardly keep my head above water and I often felt that I was going under. However, the Lord does not wrap us up in cotton wool when we make that decision to follow him but promises to be with us as an ever-present help in times of trouble.

Alongside all this stuff going on, our daughter Siân and her husband, Dan, were on the receiving end of unkind accusations linked to a conversation being misheard or misreported by others. This was painful. I find it so much harder to see my family get hurt than being hurt myself. I'm sure that I am not alone in feeling this way. Actually, I'm quite resilient when I'm the target, but if my family is targeted then I am like a lioness protecting her cubs against some dangerous predator.

Jesus told us that when a brother or sister offends you, to go and have a word with them, just between the two of you. Don't bring other people into it. Don't gossip to others. Don't act the martyr. Just talk, and do so with kindness, not to win an argument, but to be reconciled with that offending brother or sister (see Matt. 18:15-20). When Jesus' teaching is circumvented, it brings misery and heartache. When things are done the Jesus way, people — people just like Siân and Dan — then get an opportunity to either put the record straight or apologise, but when other people are brought into the story everything gets really messed up.

The result of these accusations was that they walked away from our church when, as newly-weds, they most needed the love and support of their church family. Julie and I were broken-hearted and frequently lost sleep over their plight. I would often go downstairs in the middle of the night to read, work and pray

Following a couple of years' absence from church, occasionally visiting other churches, but more often than not rejecting corporate worship for anything else that took their fancy, they returned and were reconciled with those who hurt them. They chose neither self-pity nor blame. They simply reached out without any bitterness or malice. How radical is that? I cannot say that they felt any warm feelings of beneficent goodwill, though they might have, but they made a choice, a decision that would change their future. Their decision to deal with a dire situation in "the Jesus way" brought them back into the fold, and also taught them to trust Jesus and his values. They soon became involved in ministry with young adults, and a few years later Dan was invited on to eldership and afterwards to join me on pastoral staff. He is presently doing magnificent work, ably supported by Siân.

It was in this dark time that my father was diagnosed with inoperable lung cancer and was given a limited time to live. My parents and siblings all lived in Swansea, but Julie and I lived in the Midlands, about three hours away. We visited as regularly as leading a very busy church and Julie's teaching job would allow during the next 18 months before my dad passed away. My dad died just three months after my parents had celebrated their Golden Wedding Anniversary together with their four children, twelve grandchildren and partners. My dad was a good man.

By this time, I was feeling pretty burned out and was graciously offered a three-month sabbatical by our eldership team early in 2009. This was my first and only sabbatical in over 30 years of ministry, but it couldn't have come at a better time. Many pastors take time out to visit other churches or travel abroad in a sabbatical, but that wasn't for me. A few months previously I had signed up to studying for a doctorate in ministry with Bangor University, Wales, and I saw a sabbatical as a wonderful God-sent opportunity to spend 60 hours a week on theological research. Not having the responsibilities of pastoral work and church leadership enabled me to get a significant amount done. Julie was also thrilled, as I had her dinner ready each evening by the time she got home from her busy day in the classroom. Every cloud has a silver lining! The sabbatical enabled me to focus my thoughts on something other than the difficulties of pastoral life, and to spiritually recalibrate. It was massively helpful.

Later in the year — 30th September 2009 to be precise; a date which is imprinted on my mind, and not only because it was my 50th birthday — we needed to close down our community coffee shop, which was terribly upsetting for us. Although we had never expected our coffee shop to make a profit, it enabled us to meet the immediate community on a day-to-day basis and was worth the net deficit on the accounts ledger. Having said that, as a local church and charity, we did not have a bottomless pit of funding.

To choose to use our money for one ministry meant that we couldn't fund some other area of ministry. By 2008, we were filling a gap of £30k per annum, which could not be sustained. Our coffee shop, which was located in a jaded suburb, a couple of miles away from the town centre, did not have large numbers of people passing by, nor could it charge "high street" prices for its food and drinks. At times like this one asks if the closure was God's doing or if it was some mistake that we had made. What now? Was there any future for these premises that had been such a useful resource in our doing God's work in the community of Glascote? The one thing that I could say with certainty was the sadness I felt every time I walked past the shop, all empty and forlorn with its lights turned off. These years were difficult, but then again, as that great Pentecostal pioneer, Smith Wigglesworth, used to say, "Great faith is the product of great fights. Great testimonies are the outcome of great tests. Great triumphs can only come out of great trials." So, maybe the Lord did have something more for us in days to come?

Despite the many struggles and tough times we experienced over these four or five years, the church continued to grow in ones and twos, slowly but surely. And during this time there were the occasional moments when God really showed up in quite spectacular ways, such as in Nadine's story.

It was an ordinary Sunday morning when, during Communion, I gave an invitation for people to receive prayer. A young lady whom I had not seen before approached me and Sue, one of our elders, to pray for her. She was pregnant and distressed. She told us that a recent scan had revealed that her baby was severely brain-damaged. As I remember, we prayed for her, rather boldly, asking that God would heal the baby. Sue, who has a delightful, disarming and sensitive personality, quoted in her prayer Psalm 139, verses 13 and 14, where we are told that God knows a baby during formation in the womb: "For you created my inmost being and knit me together in my mother's womb. I praise you because I am fearfully and wonderfully made."

After the service Nadine left and we heard nothing from her for a while until she sent an email to me via the church website. It stated that

God had wonderfully answered those prayers and her baby had been healed. Nadine wrote that the baby was 100% healthy and a subsequent high-resolution scan had revealed that all original problems had miraculously disappeared.

At the time of our praying we were not aware of the full extent of the problems, and it was only in an email sometime later that Nadine informed us, "I remember sitting in that cold, dark room as the Consultant hovered over me with the ultrasound in hand, clearly pointing out the hydrocephalus, missing heart valves and massive nuchal fold. This would be no ordinary baby." Nadine had great faith in God, asked for prayer, and she was rewarded with an astounding answer.

Sue kept in touch with Nadine and a short time later she received a phone call to say that baby Gabriela (Gabbi) had been born, fit and healthy. Praise God for his amazing grace, but there's more. Gabbi was a bright little girl and, when she started school, was recognised to be "gifted and talented".

More recently Nadine and her family relocated to Spain, and Gabbi quickly adapted to life and school there. Her teachers were amazed at her ability to learn two new languages fluently in under three months. The school sent her for I.Q., psychological and aptitude tests. These were repeated three times as Gabbi's results were simply off the scale. She was two to three years ahead of her peers. The Consultant had been right: she was no "ordinary" baby.

Nadine rightly insists that all glory goes to God and she uses every opportunity to witness to teachers and psychologists that Gabbi's gifting is because of a miracle God performed ten years ago. At the time of the prayer for healing, only Nadine was a Christian, and since then her whole family — husband Fernando, Gabbi's older brother Fernando junior and Gabriela herself — have come to faith. Praise be to our God "who is able to do immeasurably more than all we ask or imagine, according to his power that is at work within us" (Eph. 3:20).

POSTSCRIPT

In writing to Nadine for permission to include Gabriela's story in *Grace and Glory*, she responded with an update.

Just this weekend, Gabriela asked me to explain the miracle surrounding her development and what joy I had reminiscing and feeling the overwhelming grace of our precious Father, all over again. She is a deep, sensitive soul and hearing the story again has really touched her. It is so very humbling. She is now in her final year of primary school here in Spain, and so far for the last 2 years, she has obtained 100% for each and every subject, including Castellano and the regional dialect Valenciano. The teachers have never, ever experienced this in all their teaching years. She is a hard worker and sometimes puts too much pressure on herself to maintain this ridiculously high standard, she has problems socially and we've had our fair share of bullies (girls can be so cruel!) but she is very grounded and an incredible blessing. Every time she brings home her report, it brings me to my knees and the tears just flow.

Lord,

We have to admit that we struggle with some episodes in our lives! We cry out with the Psalmist of old, "How long, Lord? Will you forget me forever?" Help us to always lean on you during these trials, Lord, and learn to trust you more.

We pray for those we know who are currently suffering oppression or grief or illness or some other trial. May they know your miraculous touch upon their lives, and while the storms linger, let them see a sprinkling of your light in the midst of their anguish and remember that even the most tempestuous waves and squalid winds must succumb to your voice when you choose to speak!

We thank you for the astounding story of Gabbi and pray that her testimony will cause faith to rise in all who hear it, and that you will be honoured through it for many years to come.

Amen.

*"Miracle girl" Gabriela, with mum Nadine, dad Fernando,
and big brother Fernando Jnr.*

CHAPTER NINETEEN

Better Times

I will exalt you, LORD,
*   for you lifted me out of the depths*
*   and did not let my enemies gloat over me*
...
weeping may stay for the night,
*   but rejoicing comes in the morning.*
...
Hear, LORD, and be merciful to me;
*   LORD, be my help.*
You turned my wailing into dancing;
*   you removed my sackcloth and clothed me with joy,*
that my heart may sing your praises and not be silent.
*   LORD my God, I will praise you forever.*

Psalm 30:1,5,10-12

HE IS THE ONE WHO TRANSFORMS OUR WAILING INTO
dancing, who removes our sackcloth and clothes us with joy, and the One
who lifts us out of the depths. He is Lord of all. How we despise those
times when all we seem to do is weep, but during those times we need to
encourage our hearts that "rejoicing comes in the morning". We had
experienced four or five years of hardship and disappointment. After the
years of spiritual plenty, these were years of famine, times when the storm
clouds appeared and when greyness prevailed.

That season, however, was just that — a season! Thank God.

Three years after the coffee shop had closed, we decided to host a
foodbank under the auspices of the Trussell Trust, a social franchise of
some 420 foodbanks in over 1,200 centres in the UK.[17] For us, the big

---

[17] At the time of writing in winter 2018/9.

day was 7th October 2011 when Tamworth Foodbank was to open in the Manna House centre, where the coffee shop had formerly resided. This was a big deal for us. In the months of preparation for Tamworth Foodbank there were those in our town who were rather cynical. Some were saying that Tamworth, a town of 80,000 people, didn't need a foodbank, as foodbanks were for large cities, with significant poverty and homelessness.

The setting up of our foodbank was extremely challenging as there were a number of things that needed to be done concurrently. To commence a foodbank it was necessary, excuse the obvious, to have a good supply of food. To have food we needed to advertise that we were opening soon and to ask for donations from our town. To receive food we also needed somewhere to store it. We also needed to train a team of volunteers to meet and greet those who required food. Even if all this could be achieved — food donors plus storage plus volunteers — we still needed partner organisations (statutory, community, charity, churches, and schools across the town) to refer to us people who needed food. All aspects of setting up this project needed to be worked on simultaneously, which was a challenge.

We had an empty former coffee shop which became our distribution centre — the place where people came for food. The Tamworth Community Fire Station heard of our plans of opening a foodbank and with amazing generosity offered us a large brick-built external store, free of charge, for all our food stocks. They have been an amazing support since the very first day of operation. Our operations manager was Lynn, a lady who had recently retired from primary school administration, so she was not fazed by paperwork, and the warehousing was headed up by Jim, an ex-warehouseman who had also just retired. Jim retired in June and we commenced in October. Both Lynn and Jim were a God-send. Any project is only as good as the people that serve it. The writing of newspaper features, meeting council leaders, training new volunteers, taking school assemblies and the like, was left to me — essentially being the public face of Tamworth Foodbank — but my job was comparatively easy compared to that of Jim and Lynn. Jim served for five years and at the age of 70 handed over the running of the warehousing operations to Paul, a former social worker who retired early — another God-send. I would like to encourage healthy retirees that they don't need to spend every day of their later years on a golf course, or watching daytime television. There is work to be done, kingdom work, and their God-given health and spare time can be used for the purposes of God. Presently, we have over thirty superb volunteers serving those in need of food.

Seeing the old coffee shop being used again brought us such joy. The lights were on, the doors open, and there was life in the old place once more, and to use the premises for the purpose of giving food away to those who could not afford to put food on the tables for their families was especially rewarding. The generosity of local people was astonishing. Foodbank donation bins were placed in a number of churches, the town's council offices, and Morrison's and Sainsbury's supermarkets. Apart from donation bins, many kindly individuals — sometimes those who appeared not to have two pennies to rub together — came with a bag of food, often saying that when they were doing their weekly shop they felt compelled to donate to those who were worse off than themselves. It was a privilege to meet such wonderful people and also very humbling. Some others set up standing orders to help with the costs of running Tamworth Foodbank. Throughout the last seven years it has been wonderful to have such support from local people. I often refer to Tamworth Foodbank as a project which is run by the people of Tamworth for the people of Tamworth.

Each autumn, our warehouses are overflowing with food, both at our local Fire Station and our second warehouse, also supplied free of charge, by our local council. Schools throughout the town donate all their harvest produce to Tamworth Foodbank, and request our team to lead harvest assemblies. One senior school, each year, manages to fit their entire school into a sports hall, over a thousand students in all, to celebrate harvest, with either me or members of our team as guests. Whilst our desire is to meet people's needs, the ancillary message is that the Church is very much alive and kicking in Tamworth, reaching out to the poor and disenfranchised, and winning commendation from the community as we do so. Projects like foodbanks capture people's hearts and declare that Christians are people who seek to make a real difference in our world.

In 2013, we won the local newspaper's charity of the year, which was quite a prestigious award locally. *The Tamworth Herald* is a great supporter of Tamworth Foodbank and their free publicity helped put us on the map. Most people were very approving of our aims to help those on the margins of society, and we were commended in all sectors, though we were often told that it was sad that people needed to resort to having food handouts in the UK in this day and age. I could see their point. As far as I remember, there was only one disagreeable conversation over our foodbank. The organiser of a local sports club telephoned me at home one evening. He said that his particular club wished to donate food as long as we could guarantee that it would all go to "Tamworth" people. I thought I was hearing things. In shock, I asked him what he meant. He said that those donating did not want the food "going to foreigners". I attempted to clarify his statement by asking if he meant people from Wales, like me. However, the irony was lost on him. I explained that food would be given to everyone who is in need, irrespective of race, ethnicity or anything else. I desperately tried to keep my cool, and just about managed to restrain myself, but informed him that we would not be accepting food donations from his club as the conditions were not acceptable to us. What I really wanted to say was... (No! Let's not go there!)

Over the years, it has been a joy and privilege to talk to people about our ministry to the poor. In reaching out to the poor, we are following an apostolic mandate. When Paul and Barnabas met with those "esteemed as pillars" of the Jerusalem church — James, Cephas and John — and were commissioned to take the message of Christ to the Gentiles, Paul informs us that all the Jerusalem leaders requested was that Paul and Barnabas should continue to remember the poor. Paul respond-ed by declaring that it was "the very thing I had been eager to do all along" (Gal. 2:10).

I have always been totally up-front about our Christian motivation and the reasons why we do what we do. Of course, our desire is to meet real needs in society, which is reason enough to be involved in Tamworth Foodbank, but we cannot get away from the fact that our driving force is our faith in Christ. He is our motivation. I am not saying for a moment that irreligious people are not motivated altruistically to help the needy for a range of personal motivations. They are. Some of them serve in foodbanks up and down the country, including ours. There are many wonderful people around who have never darkened the doors of a church — but our motivation is Jesus, the One who has transformed our lives and has given us a heart of compassion toward the poor and needy, and we make no apology for that. I have had the opportunity to speak about my faith in the context of serving my community in schools, colleges, churches, charitable organisations like the Round Table and even at the council chambers.

"There are three kinds of lies: lies, damned lies and statistics" is a quote attributed to the 19th century British Prime Minister, Benjamin Disraeli. This phrase describes the persuasive power of numbers, particularly the use of statistics, to bolster weak arguments. One only needs to watch BBC's *Question Time* with political figures of different shades using government statistics in an attempt to "prove" their contrasting arguments, often leaving the viewers' heads in a spin.

In a church context, the most often quoted statistic focuses on the number of bottoms found on church seats during a Sunday morning service. Don't get me wrong, I think that it is important for Christians to worship together regularly, and a growing church can be a sign of church health, but it is by no means the only sign. I'm going to attempt to be a little bit more holistic for a few paragraphs, so hold on to your hat!

Over the last 25 years, Tamworth Elim Church and our Manna House charity have been privileged to serve Tamworth to the tune of 250,000 volunteer hours (a conservative estimate!), which equates to 10,000 hours per annum or approximately 200 volunteer hours per week.

Our most recent (2018) volunteer statistics are much higher, with volunteers offering over 400 hours (the equivalent of ten full-time staff members) every week to serve in tots' groups, elderly luncheon clubs, foodbank, community coffee shop, youth groups, children's clubs, shelters for the homeless *etc.* If these volunteer hours were paid at the new national living wage, it would be the equivalent of contributing £3,132 to the local economy each and every week. In addition to an army of volunteers, Elim Church / Manna House also supplies over 30 jobs for local people, further aiding the local economy.

Foodbank, which is one of our more well-known local projects, has given away to date over 140 tonnes of food since its inception in 2011. This equates to over 55,000 days of food being given away to about 17,000 people. This is quite an impressive statistic given that there were some who believed that there was no need for a foodbank in Tamworth at all!

However, it is one thing to quote statistics of volunteer helpers and of those they are helping, but beyond the numbers we need to remind ourselves that every statistic is a human being — a mother, father, brother, sister, son, daughter, grandparent — flesh and blood, people just like us, with the same material and emotional needs! Each community group or charity is inspired by some story, ideal or leader. We are no different, being motivated by the words of someone who said, "Do to others as you would have them do to you." Pretty cool saying, don't you think?

As someone once said, "Volunteering is the ultimate exercise in democracy. We vote in elections maybe once a year, but when we volunteer, we vote every day about the kind of community we want to live in."

Nine months after using the former coffee shop to host Tamworth Foodbank on a couple of afternoons each week, the church leaders made a decision to re-open the coffee shop which had laid dormant for the best part of three years. I remember the meeting well. I took a deep breath, held my nerve, and suggested that we open the coffee shop again, but this time we would give all the food and drinks away free of charge. There was an immediate gasp from my fellow leaders, followed very quickly by laughter. Good laughter. Not the kind of nervous laughter of Abraham's wife Sarah when she was told by an angel that she needed to prepare the nursery in her 90th year, but a holy laughter, a chuckling that was actually quite infectious. Within two minutes everyone had agreed that this is what we should do, and we were ready to move on to the next item on the agenda. It was astonishing. At some leadership meetings we spent considerable time debating items of far less importance, but on this occasion we all got the same vision.

We all loved the idea of giving food and drink away, free of charge, mirroring the love of God which has come to us free of charge, *gratis*, no strings attached. Many people struggle to believe that there is such a thing as a free lunch in this world. *Surely, there must be a catch,* they say. *There has to be some payback, something to contribute and something that is required of us. Quid pro quo.* We are often told that if something appears to be too good to be true, then you can pretty much guarantee that it is. You don't get something for nothing. This is the way that society views things, but we desired to be counter-cultural and be living examples of God's grace. The eldership team loved the idea. We couldn't wait to tell the rest of the church what we had decided. We knew that they would be as excited as us. I will talk a bit more about our approach to finances for church and charity in chapter 21.

Previously, our former coffee shop couldn't succeed financially when we were charging our customers, but now we had decided to actually give all our food and drink away free. How was that going to work? Well, we decided that we would only employ one person part-time and invite volunteers to come and serve in the shop. When we asked who we might employ as part-time manager, we in unison responded, "Judith." Judith had actually come to faith through an Alpha Course that was hosted in the previous coffee shop. She was as kindly, compassionate and patient a person as you would ever meet. She would be brilliant, and indeed she has been. If you remember, Judith was the lady who asked her architect husband, Bob, to help with our church plans, and who himself came to trust in Jesus.

In the former shop one could purchase a selection of fancy coffees, bacon butties and even a three-course meal, but this time round we were going to focus on simple meals, like beans on toast, and soups with a bread roll, and cakes. Rather than focus on the quality of the gastronomic experience, as previously, we wanted to focus on the friendship and the offer of a listening ear to the lonely. A local businessman, unconnected with the church, heard of our plans and offered to pay Judith's salary, which he has continued to do for a number of years, for which we are so incredibly grateful. A bakery chain from the town centre also offered cakes, pasties, sausage rolls and baguettes which hadn't been purchased by the close of their working day. It helped them in not adding to landfill and helped us to provide a greater selection of foods for our customers.

Many who have become regular customers at the Manna House Coffee Shop are those who would not have the disposable income to purchase a coffee in popular high street chains. They are people often shunned and rejected by society, but are offered love, good food and a listening ear with us. There are times, however, when our love needs to be "tough love" as some craftily attempt to exploit our kindness! Alongside the coffee shop runs a children's clothing shop which sells new and nearly new quality clothes, probably selling at less than 10% of the price of department stores. The bottom line is that we will never sell any item that we would not put on our own children or, in my case, grandchildren.

Unlike the food and drinks, we do charge for clothes, and we have two reasons for doing so. Firstly, we don't wish to rob people of their dignity. To purchase an item, even at a small cost, is more honourable than being given a "freebie". Secondly, if all the items were free of charge, experience tells us that we would get some "wise" character coming in and taking a bin-liner full of items to then sell on eBay. What did Jesus say about being as "wise as serpents and as innocent as doves"? (Matt. 10:16). Even though we decided to put a price on clothing, we have an unwritten policy that where we detect real hardship, we will happily give clothes away free of charge.

Earlier in this book I spoke of an equation that brings about maximum impact. That is, close proximity plus clear communication plus authentic living equals maximum impact. Well, our coffee shop ministry allows us that close proximity with ordinary Tamworth people on a day-to-day basis. We meet people from all walks of life, especially those who are down on their luck and have struggled at the basement of society. We cannot meet all the needs in society, but we can make a start. It's very much the principle demonstrated in that great old story of a young lad walking on a beach, where he started throwing starfish back into the sea. They had been swept up on the beach by the waves but were now drying out in the sunshine. An old man passing by said, "Son, you are not making any difference, as there are thousands of starfish on the beach." The lad smiled, bent down, picked up another starfish that he threw back into the sea, and then said to the old man, "I've just made a difference to that one!" That is essentially how we see things. We are focused on making a difference where we can, to the ones and the twos, which soon become twenties and thirties and then hundreds. Over the years, we give thanks to God that he has allowed us to impact the lives of thousands of local people with God's grace.

A few years back, I remember reading a news bulletin that ran the extraordinary story of a Northampton grandmother who tackled a gang of six robbers who were, in broad daylight, breaking into a jeweller's shop, armed with sledgehammers. The robbery was in full swing when the valiant granny ran up the street and then plunged into the gang, swinging her handbag, causing the robbers to run to the safety of their getaway scooters. Two of the men were so unsettled by this unlikely crime fighter that they overturned their scooter as they attempted to flee. Onlookers, encouraged by the woman's courage, came to her aid, which brought about the immediate arrest of four of the six gang members. Whilst most people would question the wisdom of her spur-of-the-moment reaction, her reason for responding so recklessly was, in her own words, "because somebody had to do something".

Whatever our views concerning her actions, we need to admire her "bottle" and her desire to not look the other way or stand back passively, but to do what she could. I am reminded of the story that Jesus told of a man who was severely beaten up by robbers and left for dead. Two passers-by, men who were renowned and respected by the establishment, passed by on the other side of the road, possibly thinking that should they hang around, they too would be mugged. Then, another man, a despised foreigner, someone who was an unlikely source of help, stopped and offered assistance (see Luke 10:25-37). Every week, we all meet people who are victims of life's calamities and crises, as well as encountering examples of injustice and inequality. The big questions are: Do we observe from a distance as many did in that Northampton street? Do we avert our eyes as we cross the road as did those two men in Jesus' story? Or, do we follow the example of that plucky and audacious grandmother, who was not prepared to passively accept the situation she encountered, but acted "because somebody had to do something".

I believe it is possible to observe the great needs in society and in our world and become so overwhelmed by tragedy and pain that we feel that we can do nothing to make a difference. Therefore, almost like a rabbit frozen to the spot when encountering the headlights of oncoming traffic as it attempts to cross a motorway, we freeze and do nothing, excusing ourselves by saying that we cannot make any real difference. Please don't believe that lie. We all can make a difference in a small way. Let's be courageous, as was our handbag-swinging grannie. Her boldness not only made a direct difference in bringing the criminals to justice but would have undoubtedly had a catalytic effect on the onlookers, who would have been inspired and emboldened to follow her example. Do you know that you can be a motivator for a chain-reaction of goodness?

Following the fallow years, it was good to again witness the blessing of God on our efforts for his kingdom's cause. The blessing of new, fruitful ministries was wonderfully encouraging alongside some great family blessings such as the arrival of two grandchildren, Amélie and Elijah, who have brought such great joy to Julie and me. Our grandkids are such a reward! I've often said that grandchildren are a reward for not murdering your kids and I imagine that many parents have probably come close during those "wonderful" teenage years! Let's be serious: we have three great kids and are immensely proud of them all. Around this time, I also got my doctoral dissertation written, external oral examination (*viva*) taken, and graduation, which was a very special day, especially for someone who up to the age of 25 had never read a book, of any sort. I still have a giggle to myself at the thought of it!

Lord,

Help us to shape our communities by the way we choose to live. Let us keep in mind the words of Jesus, "Do to others as you would have them do to you," as we go about our day-to-day routines, and not fall into the trap of thinking that our own business is more important than the needs of others.

Forgive us for the times we've neglected people because we've been too wrapped up in ourselves and our work. We thank you for the joy that comes through people working together for the good of the whole community. We thank you for seasons of blessing and fulfilment and pray that we will draw strength and spiritual nourishment from such times that will sustain us through more difficult moments.

Amen.

CHAPTER TWENTY

Changing of the Guard

FOR A NUMBER OF YEARS, MY ASSOCIATE PASTOR, PAUL, AND I had discussed how to bring some new and younger leaders on to the team. We were both conscious of getting older, and therefore not being entirely representative of our church family anymore. I was at this time in my early 50s and Paul four years older than me. God had it all sorted, as ever. Paul, an ordained Elim pastor, was invited to accept a pastorate in Birmingham, which he was thrilled to do, and became a blessing to his new church. Although sorry to see him leave, his move opened up new possibilities for us at Tamworth.

We were initially looking to fill a role which was part pastoral and part administrative so invited Jackie, an old friend of Julie's and mine from Swansea. We all belonged to the same youth group, would you believe? Jackie had studied at Regents Theological College and worked as the college registrar for many years before serving as a missionary in Malawi and then in Haiti following the awful earthquake of 2010. Jackie had been wounded through her missionary experiences and was quite burned out at the time. I'm glad that she was willing to come to Tamworth, because I knew that such a loving church community would help breathe new life back into her. She was a great help in both administration and pastoral work, though I didn't expect her to stay with us in the longer term as I could see that she had Africa in her blood. Her stay was indeed short-lived, 18 months in all, but during that time Jackie had time to heal, aided by the love of the Tamworth church family. It was our pleasure to become her "sending" church, and also to support her financially when the time came for her to go and work in Malawi once again. Our links continue to be strong.

Following Jackie's departure, the leaders of the church wanted to invite a younger person into leadership. The post was advertised widely, with applicants as far away as the USA. However, the answer was found much closer at home, in the person of my son-in-law, Dan. When Dan, who was already a church elder, told me that he had decided to apply, I immediately took a step back and asked the eldership team to take care of the appointment. They were more than capable. They also invited our Regional Leader to be involved, which was a wise move. I not only wanted to do the right thing, but be seen to do the right thing, and not have any allegations of nepotism. The right decision, I believe, was made, and Dan was invited to join me in pastoral oversight of our church. Dan also took the opportunity to finish a degree in theology that he had started a number of years before when he served as a church youth worker.

I knew that Dan had certain gifts and abilities, but anticipated that I would need to spoon-feed him for a while. Nothing could have been further from the truth. He has grown into the role with remarkable anointing. He has great ability and a pastor's heart. It thrills me to see a younger leader flourish as he has, thus far.

At the conclusion of the so-called "tough" years, I made a decision, which at the time I could not have envisaged would have been quite so significant. One day, in the summer of 2011, I chatted to a couple of our school leavers who had just completed their A-levels: Brenda, a South African who had emigrated from the "rainbow nation" with her parents and brother a few years earlier; and Amy, a Tamworth girl through and through. Neither had any real idea what they wanted to do next with their lives, and neither had the means, or probably the desire, to attend university. I felt quite sorry for them, as I do for many school leavers who are required to make such big decisions which will have a significant impact on their futures.

To cut a long story short, I asked them to consider becoming interns with our church. Looking back, the conversation just seemed so right. Even as I chatted with them, I was conscious that I was making up the script as I went along. I told them that I didn't have any model to follow, or how every detail would pan out, but I suggested that if they were interested in becoming interns, we could pay them essentially what amounted to pocket-money, and also pay for them to do a Bachelor of Arts degree in applied theology with Regents Theological College, in Malvern, which is our Movement's college. They could participate in the distance-learning option which would allow them to study part-time and also gain experience in a whole host of community programmes — working in schools, with children and youth, learning the ropes in a busy day nursery, working with the elderly, *etc.* I also suggested that at the end of their first year, we would finance a missions trip with an organisation like Open Doors that works with, and on behalf of, the persecuted church. I could see many benefits for this arrangement — benefits for them and for us. Such a scheme would allow them to get UK degrees, whilst gaining valuable work experience and being debt-free. Our "win" was that we would have talented and committed young people working on a number of our projects throughout the week. I spoke to the leadership team about this concept and they loved it. Phew! Throughout my life and ministry, I have lived with the mindset of it being better to ask for forgiveness than for permission. But again, that statement needs to be understood in the context of having fellow leaders who are also "possibility thinkers" — people who think of church and ministry creatively.

Roll on seven years: we now have both Brenda and Amy employed full-time in children's and youth ministries. After the first year of internship, we sent them both to Egypt with Open Doors. It was quite a life-changing experience for them to witness what it was like for many of their fellow Christians living under persecution. At this time, Amy asked us if she could be released from the internship to work with our day nursery. We gladly obliged and allowed her to build a career as a nursery nurse, gaining all the necessary qualifications. Brenda, on the other hand, displayed great ability with "children and schools" work. Brenda continued on the internship for a couple more years and in recognition of her obvious gifting, we employed her as our children's worker. As an employee, she carried on with her studies, self-funding the remainder of her course. We were so impressed with her pastoral and leadership ability that we then invited her to become our children's pastor just before she concluded her distance-learning degree, six years on.

Up until this time, the children's ministry had been led by Bev Marshall, who came to faith as an 11-year-old in the late 1970s at a Sunday School outreach of our church on a local housing estate. Bev is an amazing children's worker who has lived and breathed children's work since long before we met her. She is blessed with a disarming personality and a wicked sense of humour. Her passion for this work has not waned over time, and today she continues to work alongside Brenda. Bev's full-time employment restricted her from being involved in schools work, so to have Brenda working with her was such a blessing. We are so fortunate to have Bev, Brenda and other wonderfully talented children's workers.

More recently, Amy was invited to move away from her nursery role to become a full-time youth worker, a role in which she excels. Having such talented young people, whose heart and soul is in serving God within the context of their own local church, is a blessing. Both Amy and Brenda have remarkable maturity and wisdom for those who are so young. Their roles are very important to our community ministry that has a significant focus on young people. Each Friday evening, we host a children's ministry that is largely aimed at children of families that don't attend church. Our KidzKlub, ably led by Nick and Deborah, two more amazing children's leaders, is a 21st century version of the Sunday School of my childhood years, but a lot more fun. The children enjoy a full range of fun games, activities and Bible lessons. A year before they finish primary school, around the age of ten, they are invited to join our youth group. Transferring children from children's groups to youth groups, especially if they are from non-church-attending homes, is a significant challenge for all churches. We, at all costs, need to think through our strategy to cause this transition to be as smooth and seamless as possible. Many churches manage well-attended children's ministries but fail at the next stage, which is considerably more challenging. We are not experts, by a long way, but we seek to be relevant and to create a loving, fun and faith-filled community.

It is an immense privilege for me to observe quality younger people taking up the challenge of serving God, and an even greater privilege for me to be involved, in some small way, in their spiritual development and training. For many years now, I have been aware that discipleship training isn't purely a classroom activity or about head-knowledge, but life-transformation. Classes do not create mature believers; they create bright believers. Don't get me wrong; I think that theological education is wonderful and have a couple of higher theological degrees to prove it, but theological education and spiritual maturity are not necessarily the same thing. Our desire at Tamworth Elim is to lead people into a growing relationship with Jesus, which will obviously include knowledge of the Bible, but is even more about a person's growing confidence in God and the fuelling of their faith.

What makes a disciple of Christ? Answer: a diverse mix of things. Yes, it will include having a greater knowledge of the Bible, and especially where the biblical text is being applied to all aspects of one's life, but there are other elements too which I will move on to in a moment. Firstly, however, let me tell you a few things about our main Sunday celebration service, which we see as an important opportunity to teach our church family how to read, understand and apply Bible truths.

Throughout the year, we have a varied diet of scriptural teaching. We regularly focus on teaching about the ministry of the church in the early part of the year (ecclesiology). Then towards Easter, we often have a more devotional emphasis, focusing on the events leading up to Good Friday and Easter Sunday. In the summer term, we teach a longer, expository series on a New Testament book, leaving no stone unturned. The last few years we have focused on a different letter of Paul's each summer. During the autumn, we have a punchier series, like an apologetics series on *Big Questions* or *Stories Old and New*, focusing on the parables of Jesus and contemporary stories. Most series last six to eight weeks, with the summer term New Testament series often lasting longer — three or four months. Much in the way that you want a variety in your diet — you wouldn't want to be eating fish and chips every day, even if it is your favourite meal — we similarly offer a broad "spiritual" diet to our church family and many have found this approach helpful to their spiritual growth. I think that biblical illiteracy is a problem in British society, where a significant majority of new converts have next to zero biblical knowledge. Christian foundations in British society have long since crumbled in a secular age and, apart from in some church schools, Christianity is regarded as a quaint and antiquated memorial of a by-gone age for many. Since this is the case, I've found that the expository series in a New Testament book is particularly helpful as we essentially take the whole congregation by the hand and walk them through the text week by week dealing with whatever subject comes next in the Scriptures. This has provided many of our church family with a new confidence to read the Scriptures for themselves.

At Tamworth Elim, we do our best not to talk in biblical jargon or use theological terminology, nor do we have a desire to show how theologically "switched on" or "sound" we are, but have great passion to make the Bible accessible to the entire congregation that has widely diverse backgrounds and education. We work really hard on this. Our church family then has opportunity to work through the Sunday teaching via their life groups during the week, which is where the Sunday teaching really takes root and is worked out in people's lives. We recognise that our teaching needs to be not simply *true* but also *helpful* to the daily lives of our church family.

Furthermore, we encourage our church family to read the Scriptures and to take time to replenish their hearts through personal study and prayer. American megachurch pastor Andy Stanley states that "there is a direct correlation between a person's private devotional life and his or her personal faith"[18], and I think he is correct. We recognise that there is only so much that can be done through church meetings in aiding believers to excel in their devotional lives. A baby will grow into a toddler and then into a child who can use cutlery properly — eventually, though often not soon enough for most parents. It would be misguided of us to think that spoon-feeding is for life. Similarly, a spiritual "baby" might be helped to digest the strong meat of Christian theology for a season, but there needs to come a time when she needs to feed herself. To extend the metaphor, she needs to find her own feet as a Christian believer, and when this starts to happen, we see accelerated spiritual growth.

As with our former interns, Brenda and Amy, we have a strong desire to allow people to explore their gifting as Christian believers, often inviting them to serve in some Christian ministry before they are ready. This sometimes backfires on us for obvious reasons, but for the most part we observe spiritual growth in those who are challenged to spiritually step up into some area of service.

I am conscious that providing new believers with appropriate opportunities for service can be an area of great challenge for many churches, especially if they are churches that meet solely for the purpose of worship or Bible teaching. When I became a follower of Jesus in the late 1970s, I had the opportunity to help with Sunday School or a boys' club. All church ministries were confined to the four walls of the church and there were no opportunities to work with, for example, the homeless or elderly, the poor or the addict; besides which, I always got the feeling that such works outside the church building were never regarded as quite as "spiritual" as what happened within. In those days, many of my evangelical/Pentecostal friends cautioned against what they considered to be the social gospel, which is no gospel at all! I was told that the greatest need is spiritual — people need Christ. Agreed! But they also needed

---

[18] Stanley, A., *Deep & Wide,* Grand Rapids, Zondervan, 2012, 117.

feeding and friendship and to be loved and accepted as people created and loved by God, not just potential "converts". Feeding the poor never felt quite as spiritual as leading a Bible study or prayer meeting in those days. I am encouraged that many these days have a more holistic message of good news to society.

One of the benefits of an incarnational model of church, and our church in particular, is that ministry isn't merely focused on what happens in the four walls of a church building, or in the context of some kind of Bible teaching, whether to adults or to children — ministry is considerably more diverse, and as new Christians get involved in serving in some community project or ministry we witness accelerated spiritual growth. I have also found that when people talk about key moments on their spiritual journeys, they often speak of the first time that they got involved in some area of ministry, a time when they were forced to be dependent on God, as a major contributing factor.

I also believe that strong relationships are important to Christian discipleship. I have heard many church leaders say that it is one thing to get a person through the front doors of a church, but it is their relationship with their fellow Christians that will prevent them from leaving through the back door. I agree, but I would also add that those relationships, especially if they are with mature, loving, gracious believers, are a critical factor in their spiritual development. The Alpha Course is a quite brilliant tool for introducing people to the Christian faith — the video materials are exceptional — yet the real "genius" of Alpha is the opportunity to sit and eat food with a group of strangers who after a couple of months become friends. I have observed that "doing life" together with other like-minded people has a greater impact on spiritual growth than many a sermon preached from pulpits. I'm not sure that I enjoyed saying that!

———————————

Father God,

Thank you for the rich heritage of millions of Christians who have paved the way on the path of faith before us. Thank you, too, for the privilege and opportunity of working alongside others in various forms of ministry. We learn so much from each other, Lord.

We also recognise our need to know you more and more, and so we pray that we will always treasure time spent alone with you. Give us fresh understanding as we read our Bibles and help us to live by the principles that you have set out for our good. Help us to grow in wisdom, Father, and when the time is right, grant us the joy of handing over the batons of ministry to a new generation who are ready and eager to run the race after us.

Amen.

Changing the guard. Young leaders: Amy, Dan and Brenda (left to right).

CHAPTER TWENTY-ONE

Money, Money, Money!

THERE IS AN OLD STORY ABOUT A WELL-WORN £5 NOTE AND a rather tattered £50 note that arrived at the official Bank of England incinerator to be pulped. As they moved along the conveyor belt to be burned, they struck up a conversation. (Did I say this isn't a true story?)

The £50 note reminisced about its travels all over the world. "I've had a pretty good life," the £50 note declared. "I've been to Las Vegas and Monte Carlo, the finest restaurants in New York, performances on Broadway and even a cruise to the Caribbean."

"Wow!" said the £5 note. "You've really had an exciting life!"

"So tell me," said the £50, "where have you been throughout your lifetime?"

The £5 note replied, "Oh, I've been to the Methodist Church, the Baptist Church, the Lutheran Church and the Pentecostal Church."

The £50 note interrupted, "What's a church?"

Groan! There is a range of responses when "money" or "giving" is mentioned in a church context. Some might think of a TV evangelist playing his audience in order to fund a new jet for his worldwide ministry. Others might envision images of thermometers outside some church buildings collecting for the new roof or church organ or, perhaps, the annual jumble sale or whist drive aimed to raise money for some churchy cause. Even among practising Christians, there are some who think that to speak about money is impolite, unspiritual or crude, and that preachers should stick to more "spiritual" subjects!

Apart from his teaching on the kingdom of God, which included reference to money, Jesus taught more on the subject of money than any other; but why? The answer, I believe, is that Money is the number one rival to God for the human heart. Jesus himself declared that it was

153

impossible to love both God and Money, as they will fight for our devotion (see Matt. 6:24). The Bible teaches that God promises to fulfil all our greatest desires. It is in God that our security is to be found; in him we will find our significance and our identity as his children; it is in him that we find freedom from all that enslaves us; in him we find satisfaction and fulfilment — yet Money comes along and shouts for our attention. Money says, "Look to me and I will give you security." When we speak of having a secure future, we are speaking essentially of being financially well-off. Money subtly entices us to believe that it will make us important. "Do you want identity?" asks Money. "Then look to me, for I will allow you to purchase it; you will be able to choose the right house, in the right neighbourhood, and I will enable you to drive the right car and buy the right clothes to wear. If you want pleasure, it isn't God you need, it is me, because there is nothing that I can't buy. If it is satisfaction or fulfilment you want, then buy the next thing that your heart desires!"

It is so subtle, isn't it? Money promises those things that ultimately only God can give: security, significance, freedom, fulfilment, satisfaction, identity and pleasure, but Money's promises are superficial and short-lived. That is why, I believe, Money is the number one rival to God for the human heart and why Jesus spoke so often on this subject. Billy Graham once said, "If a person gets his attitude to money straight, it will help straighten out almost any other area of his life."[19]

Whilst on the one hand I acknowledge that Jesus often taught on money, on the other hand I have been extremely cautious, if not reticent, at times to teach on this subject myself — maybe because I have become very aware of the way that Christian giving has been portrayed and misrepresented in contemporary culture. Trying to strike the right balance is so important in church life, so let me share a few decisions or principles that I/we have made at our church, though not everyone will agree with all that I write. Anyhow, here goes...

I DON'T NEED TO KNOW

Two men were marooned on a desert island. One man paced back and forth, anxious and fearful, while the other man sat back and was sunning himself.

---

[19] *https://ym.christianleadershipalliance.org/page/billygrahamleader*

The first man said to the second man, "Aren't you afraid? We are about to die."

"No," said the second man, "I make £100,000 a week and I faithfully give 10% to my church — my pastor *will* find me!"

Right at the commencement of our ministry in Tamworth, I asked the church leadership team if they would release me from knowing anything about a person's individual giving to our church. Whilst recognising that it was important for church finances to be properly administered and accounted, and for details of Gift Aid givers to be kept, I simply didn't want to know what anyone gave to the church. I needed others to take care of that stuff. The reason: I couldn't trust myself with that knowledge. What if a poor person gave 30% or 40% of their meagre salary to the church; would I show that person preference in some manner? Conversely, and more worryingly, would I show some kind of bias against a wealthy member who might not give in proportion to his personal resources? My desire, as pastor, is to offer pastoral support and prayer, without discrimination, to each and every member of the church family, irrespective of how much they might contribute financially. I had no desire to be swayed either towards or against a church member based on their giving. The prophet Jeremiah was speaking about me, and possibly you too, when he declared, "The heart is deceitful above all things, and desperately wicked; who can know it?" (Jeremiah 17:9, NKJV)

That is a practice that my leadership team has allowed me to continue for the duration of my ministry, and for which I would like to thank them. This freedom has also allowed me to speak quite powerfully about money issues without anyone thinking that I am getting at them in some way.

TO TITHE OR NOT TO TITHE, THAT IS THE QUESTION!

Does God command me to tithe (give one tenth of my income)? What does the Bible teach? Are we robbing God by not tithing? Over the years, I have heard many references, if not entire sermons, on the words of the prophet Malachi: "'Will a mere mortal rob God? Yet you rob me.' But you ask, 'How are we robbing you?' 'In tithes and offerings. You are under a curse — your whole nation — because you are robbing me. Bring the whole tithe into the storehouse, that there may be food in my house. Test me in this,' says the Lord Almighty, 'and see if I will not throw open the floodgates of heaven and pour out so much blessing that there will not be room enough to store it.'" (Mal. 3:8-10)

Often in sermons, I have heard the reference of bringing the "whole tithe into the storehouse" being used to refer to giving 10% of your income to your local church. Anything over and above this initial 10%, whether to the local church or to some other Christian charities and ministries, can be regarded as a free-will offering. But is that a legitimate understanding of Scripture? Does the Old Testament (Hebrew) Law have any relevance to my life today? Hasn't the Law been superseded? Does this teaching, which was essentially akin to our modern income tax system, have any more relevance than the Levitical teaching on mildew or menstruating women? It is really important to get this question answered, because no Christian would ever wish to rob anyone — and especially not rob God.

Let's do a whistle-stop tour. If we start in the Old Testament, we will see that there are many Scriptures that teach about giving one-tenth. Even before the Law was given to Moses at Mount Sinai, we have examples of Abraham giving one-tenth of the spoils of war to the King of Salem, a mysterious man named Melchizedek, who was also referred to as a priest of "God Most High". Melchizedek blessed Abraham, and Abraham gave him a tenth of the spoils of war (Gen. 14:20). Furthermore, in Genesis 28, we read of Jacob, the grandson of Abraham, making a vow to God, that if God should give him protection and provision on his journey, he would give him a tenth of all that God has given him.

Some Christians believe that the practice of tithing, which predated the Old Testament (OT) Law, is a biblical principle that we need to embrace today. But let's be very careful here! When we read the Scriptures, especially the narrative parts (the stories!) we need to ask ourselves, is this descriptive or is it prescriptive? That is, when I read this narrative, is it just a story that sheds light on Abraham and Jacob and is therefore descriptive, i.e. describing what happened for them, or is his story included in the Bible for me to copy, i.e. prescriptive? This is a much, much bigger subject than I have the opportunity of addressing just now but a terribly important question for us to ask when we read the narrative sections in the Bible (New Testament as well as Old).

Without any doubt in my mind, this is descriptive. It describes what Abraham did and what Jacob did without even the remotest suggestion that we should follow their examples, any more than the story of Abraham and Hagar would suggest that it is permissible for childless couples to agree that the husband should have sex with the maid in order to have a child, or even that it is OK to lie, cheat and steal as Jacob did over his birthright.

Let's fast forward some hundreds of years later. Moses was given the Law, and the OT Law, which included the 10 commandments, had a number of things to say about giving. For example, "A tithe of everything from the land, whether grain from the soil or fruit from the trees, belongs to the Lord; it is holy to the Lord ... Every tithe of the herd and flock — every tenth animal that passes under the shepherd's rod — will be holy to the Lord" (Lev. 27:30,32).

Over and above the various tithes instituted in the OT Law (which amounted to over 20% of one's income) there was also a variety of freewill offerings. These freewill offerings were, as their name suggests, not compulsory, but discretionary. In fact, the Israelites on one occasion were so generous that Moses needed to stop them bringing their gifts for the building of the sanctuary (see Ex. 36:6). I've yet to hear of any pastor instructing his church congregation to stop giving because they were being too generous! If you know of such an example, please let me know.

More importantly, what does the New Testament (NT) teach about tithing, if anything? Tithing is mentioned on three occasions.

- The Pharisee in Jesus' parable prayed in the temple, "God, I thank you that I am not like other people — robbers, evildoers and adulterers — or even like this tax collector. I fast twice a week and give a tenth of all I get." The focus on this story is humility in prayer, not giving. Reference to giving a tenth is merely ancillary. See Luke 18:11-12.
- Hebrews 7:1-10 retells the OT story of Abraham giving a tenth to Melchizedek. The emphasis here is on the priesthood of Melchizedek — a mystical character that prefigured Christ — as being greater than the Levitical priesthood. Again, to suggest that this instructs followers of Christ to tithe is simply reading into the text something that isn't there.
- Jesus is recorded as saying to the religious teachers, "Woe to you, teachers of the law and Pharisees, you hypocrites! You give a tenth of your spices — mint, dill and cumin. But you have neglected the more important matters of the law — justice, mercy and

157

faithfulness. You should have practised the latter, without neglecting the former" (Matt. 23:23; see also Lk. 11:42). Some people take this verse as Jesus validating and endorsing the OT teaching of tithing when he said, "You should have practised the latter" (justice, mercy and faithfulness) "without neglecting the former" (the giving of 10%). So there it is: Jesus is teaching that we should not neglect the former, the NT does teach the giving of 10%. Not so fast! Tithing, like other old covenant rules and rituals, was a law at the time Jesus spoke. It was the law of the land. They didn't live in a democracy where they elected their own government; theirs was a theocracy, where God ruled through the Law that he gave for all manner of everyday events. Not to tithe was, in effect, to break the law. Of course they were to continue giving a tenth — Jesus would not have instructed them otherwise — but their giving the bare requirements of the Law did not mean that they could ignore the weightier matters of justice, mercy and faithfulness.

Many Christians are really confused over what the OT Law has to do with them today. The answer is *nothing* — it is obsolete and superseded. Paul tells us in his letter to Romans, "For sin shall no longer be your master, because you are not under the law, but under grace" (Rom. 6:14). In the following chapter, he then provides us with a great argument that we have died to the Law and have been released from that marriage contract. We are now married to someone else — Jesus. Our new husband is an infinitely better husband than old Mr Law ever was. The standards in the NT are very different from the OT. The Old Covenant focused on performance (on keeping the regulations and rituals, of sacrifices and tithing and the like); Jesus' performance completely satisfied his Father. The focus of the New Covenant is not on performance but on position. Paul writes to the church at Ephesus (2:14-15), "For he himself is our peace, who has made the two groups one [i.e. Jews and Gentiles] and has destroyed the barrier, the dividing wall of hostility, by setting aside in his flesh the law with its commands and regulations. His purpose was to create in himself one new humanity out of the two, thus making peace..." (Eph. 2:14-15).

So, what is the standard of giving in the NT then? Jesus never taught about how much we should give, but we find some quite startling examples of giving in the Gospels, such as the widow who placed into the Temple treasury everything she had to live on (Lk. 21:1-2) and Zacchaeus, the tax collector. His encounter with Jesus caused him to promise to give half of his possessions to the poor and to pay back four times the amount of anything he had taken dishonestly. That encounter changed his attitude to wealth and money (Lk. 19:1-10). The first century church in Jerusalem was highly esteemed as an example of those who "sold property and possessions to give to anyone who had need" (Acts 2:45) and shared their possessions, even selling them to meet the needs of their fellow Christians (Acts 4:32-37). Paul further speaks of the Christians from Macedonia (2 Cor. 8:2-3) who "in the midst of a very severe trial, their overflowing joy and their extreme poverty welled up in rich generosity. For I testify that they gave as much as they were able, and even beyond their ability..." Paul uses the Macedonian Christians as an example of how believers are to give: "Remember this: Whoever sows sparingly will also reap sparingly, and whoever sows generously will also reap generously. Each of you should give what you have decided in your heart to give, not reluctantly or under compulsion, for God loves a cheerful giver" (2 Cor. 9:6-7). There is nothing about tithing in any of these texts but a lot about generosity of spirit. There was no compulsion, as they were not under the Law, but were encouraged to give freely, which is giving in the NT way.

So, as far as Tamworth Elim is concerned, tithing is never mentioned in our teaching, but generosity is, often. No one is ever compelled or made to feel guilty or that they are a second-class citizen if they cannot or do not have the desire to give — for the Lord loves a cheerful giver. We teach that God responds to a generous heart and open-handedness, and that we will reap generously if we sow generously, without falling into the trap of the prosperity gospel that teaches that financial blessing and physical well-being are always God's will for believers. We encourage our church family to freely give just as they have freely received from the Lord. If that isn't a motivation for giving then no amount of compulsion, persuasion or coercion will make any difference.

OFFERING BASKETS OR DONATION BOXES?

Over the years, we have made some decisions regarding finance that have raised an eyebrow or two. As previously stated, it was our decision to take Lottery money for the non-religious work of our community charity. As you will remember from chapter 14 we accepted that money was neither good nor evil. The important question was what that money was used for, and we chose to use it for the benefit of people living on the margins of society, to bring support and comfort to their lives.

Another surprise came when we made the decision to open a coffee shop that was entirely free to our community. That decision remains a talking point a number of years on. The world in which we live declares there is no such thing as a free lunch, and we say, "You're wrong!" I am still tickled at the look of surprise on people's faces when they hear that they can visit our coffee shop and receive free food and drink, and that we neither expect nor desire a financial contribution. It is a great conversation-starter about God's amazing grace.

Maybe the biggest surprise of all came when we announced to our church family that we were discontinuing the Sunday offering. We made a decision to release people from the expectation to give financially, should they wish not to, and placed a donations box at the rear of the church. "But why?" you might ask. Primarily, as a church with so many community projects, which often act as a doorway into the church, we found ourselves talking about Christianity being a free gift from God and then passing the offering baskets around inviting a financial contribution to our cause. It just seemed as though we were giving a mixed message. For a while, like many other churches, we made an announcement that if a person was visiting that morning they were our guests and to allow the basket to go by *etc.*, but the whole process was clunky and clumsy, and baskets were still passed to our guests, if only to pass them on to the next person. There was an embarrassment and awkwardness about the whole thing. Furthermore, a number of our church members were discomforted by this practice too, as they never placed any money in the offering baskets because they contributed monthly by standing order, but no one else knew that! Not that anyone was watching, of course!

We took the plunge and stopped taking a church offering, and guess what? The offerings stayed the same, and soon afterwards increased. These days, we briefly explain our message about giving through our monthly newsletters so that visitors are aware of what we are doing, and should they wish to give, they know how to go about it. Two or three times each year we host a Welcome Evening for people who have decided to attend our church, or indeed for those who remain unsure about joining us, as it provides us with the opportunity to tell our story — our church history, ministries, beliefs and practices (including money issues and the benefit of gift aiding) over a meal with the leadership team. It has worked well for us.

So, essentially, we encourage our church family as Jesus taught his followers — "Freely you have received; freely give" (Matt. 10:8) — with the promise that as we give (not only speaking of finances) it will be given to us: "a good measure, pressed down, shaken together and running over, will be poured into your lap. For with the measure you use, it will be measured to you" (Lk. 6:38).

Dear Lord,

We rejoice that we serve a generous God! Your grace and love know no limits. May our lives reflect our deep gratitude for the New Life that we received freely but that cost you so much. We choose to live our lives as living sacrifices to you.

We pray that you will help us to give generously of our finances, our resources, our time and energy, not begrudgingly, but cheerfully, out of the fullness of our thankful hearts.

Amen.

CHAPTER TWENTY-TWO

Grace – Our Greatest Motivation

SO, WHY DO WE DO WHAT WE DO? WHAT HAS CAUSED US TO make all those sacrifices of time, finance and effort that you have read about in the chapters of this book? What is our driving force, our motivation? And what gets us up from bed every morning as we continue serving his purposes in his world? I'm glad that you asked!

This chapter is going to be a bit more theological! What did you expect?

For me, it all starts with God, a God who is not merely loving, but One who defines himself as love (1 Jn. 4:8,16). The way that we view God's nature is imperative to what we believe, the way our lives are lived and the manner in which our ministry is conducted. There is an important connection between God's attributes and his acts which are outflows of his nature. If God is love at his core, then those who are his followers would seek to emulate this quality, for as St. Paul writes, "...Christ's love compels us..." (2 Cor. 5:14).

The Bible reveals God as multi-dimensional. He is not just a God of love, for he is righteous, holy, faithful, just *etc.* But considerable confusion lies over the manner in which each attribute or quality of God interacts with all the others. This confusion is perhaps best illustrated by author Brian McLaren who so poignantly states that God is sometimes portrayed as suffering from "borderline personality disorder or some worse sociopathic diagnosis". McLaren, a leading figure in the so-called Emerging Church, caricatures the way that God is often depicted in contemporary Christianity: "God loves you and has a wonderful plan for your life, and if you don't love God back and cooperate with God's plans in exactly the prescribed way, God will torture you with unimaginable abuse, forever."[20] As much as I hate to admit it, I have occasionally observed this kind of neurotic "turn or burn" version of Christianity in some churches and evangelistic outreaches. Evangelical luminary John Stott spoke out against this kind of teaching on eternal conscious punishing, stating, "I find the concept intolerable and do not understand how people can live with it without either cauterizing their feelings or cracking under the strain."[21]

But is that the way that God should be understood? When I have passionately declared the love of God in sermons, I have been occasionally told, sometimes mildly rebuked, that God is also a God of justice, just in case I might veer too close to the precipice of universalism.[22] Perish the thought!

Divine justice and mercy have often been viewed as distinct, if not contrary or conflicting, characteristics often creating a "schizophrenic" view of God. So, what are we to make of this? Does God actually have competing and conflicting characteristics? Does he truly desire the salvation of humankind? If yes, then does he have the ability to bring his plans to fulfilment? Maybe the first thing we need to do is understand a little bit more about God's qualities or characteristics.

Systematic theologians can help us out here with their concept of Divine Simplicity. This is the belief that God is without parts and that his being is identical to his attributes. For example, God doesn't merely display goodness, he is goodness. He doesn't merely love, he is love. He doesn't merely act justly, he is just *etc.* So, there cannot be any suggestion that God is part love, part light, part holy and so forth. He is all of these things all of the time. Since that is the case, all his divine attributes are

---

[20] McLaren, B. D., *The Last Word and the Word After That*, San Francisco, Josey-Bass, 2005, xii.; see also Stephen Jonathan, *Grace Beyond the Grave*, Eugene, OR., Wipf and Stock, 2014, 111.

[21] Edwards D. L. and & Stott J., *Essentials: A Liberal-Evangelical Dialogue*, Downers Grove, IVP, 314. Edwards referred to the God presented in the classical view of hell as the "Eternal Torturer" which encouraged this response from Stott. See also Marshall, I. H., "The New Testament does not teach Universal Salvation," in *Universal Salvation?* edited by R. Parry and C. Partridge, Carlisle, Paternoster, 60, who believes that the view of endless, conscious suffering is irreconcilable with the love of God. See also Wenham, J., *Facing Hell: An Autobiography*, Carlisle, Paternoster, 1998, 254.

[22] Universalism, also called ultimate reconciliation, is the belief that ultimately all will be saved.

harmonious; thus, God's justice is *loving* justice and God's love is a *just* love.[23]

If God is love, as John teaches, and if love is a part of his very essence, then surely he cannot act in unloving ways towards anyone, even his enemies. On the basis of this truth, Jesus instructed his disciples to love their enemies and in doing so they would "be perfect" even as their "heavenly Father is perfect" (Matt. 5:43-48). God is love in exactly the same sense that he is light, which would mean it is as impossible for God not to love someone as it is for him to manifest darkness rather than light.[24] MacDonald argues, "If God is love, then all of God's actions must be compatible with his love. This means that his holiness is loving, his justice is loving and his wrath is loving."[25] But how does this work out? In which way can we harmonise God's attributes of love and justice? What do God's loving justice and his just love look like?[26]

Whilst it is impossible to condense a gargantuan subject (a doctoral thesis) into a few lines, it is my belief that love is the essential attribute of God, for it was out of love that God came to save the world, not to condemn it or to demonstrate his wrath on mankind. John writes, "For God did not send his Son into the world to condemn the world, but to save the world through him" (Jn. 3:17). The divine objective for the incarnation and atonement was love, not wrath. If there were no sin, there would be no wrath.[27] God's wrath is, essentially, injured love which is contingent on sin, whereas love is a permanent attribute of God, much like justice and holiness.[28]

The overarching theme of the Bible is that of God, a loving Creator, unceasingly pursuing humankind to bring it into a relationship with himself. Jesus explained to Nicodemus that "God so loved the world that

---

[23] For a full discussion on this subject, see Stephen Jonathan, *Grace Beyond the Grave*, 93-151.

[24] Talbott, *The Inescapable Love of God*, n.p. Universal, 1999, 116.

[25] MacDonald, G., *The Evangelical Universalist*, Eugene, Cascade, 103-4. Gregory MacDonald is a pseudonym for Robin Parry.

[26] For an in-depth look at this subject, see my book *Grace Beyond the Grave*, chapter 4, pages 93-151, especially my thoughts on the possibility of God's justice being restorative rather than retributive. This book is based on my doctoral work and is a tough read for those not well-acquainted with theological discourse. Be warned! It is also available on Kindle.

[27] Travis, S. H., *Christ and the Judgement of God*, Milton Keynes, Paternoster, 2008, 70.

[28] Erickson, M., *Christian Theology*, Grand Rapids, Baker, 1998, 318.

he gave his one and only Son, that whoever believes in him shall not perish but have eternal life" (Jn. 3:16). Paul wrote similarly that "God demonstrates his own love for us in this: while we were still sinners, Christ died for us" (Rom. 5:8). John likewise asserts, "This is love, not that we loved God, but that he loved us and sent his Son as an atoning sacrifice for our sins" (1 Jn. 4:10). Peter also affirms God's love to the world, a love that desires that none should perish but that everyone should come to repentance (2 Pet. 3:9).

Jesus portrayed God not just as a father but as a *good* father, infinitely superior in character and goodness to any human father. Jesus states, "Which of you, if his son asks for bread, will give him a stone? Or if he asks for a fish, will give him a snake? If you, then, though you are evil, know how to give good gifts to your children, *how much more* will your Father in heaven give good gifts to those who ask him?" (Matt. 7:9-11, my italics).

Many parents, including me, have learned more about the heart of God in their first few minutes of parenthood than through years of theological study, as they passionately desired to guard, guide and bless their children.[29] Whilst no human being would ever claim to be a faultless "textbook" parent, many would give their lives for their children and do anything and everything within their power to save their children from hurt or harm. Jesus teaches that if human parents love to bless their children with good gifts, *how much more* would Father God bless his children, thus demonstrating that God is infinitely superior?

Of course, we must be careful not to become over-self-indulgent and sentimental, portraying God as a benevolently adoring father who carries a photograph of you in his wallet and brags about you to the angelic host. Yes, I have heard this kind of overly romantic view of God proclaimed from pulpits from time to time. It works for some, though not for me, I'm afraid! Whilst it is imperative to understand, appreciate and promote the love of God, we need care not to demean his justice or discipline, for what good parent would excuse the bad behaviour of their child, or would just say yes to every request? For God to be a loving Father and a good God, his fatherly and loving discipline would be an indispensable characteristic of his being. However, one cannot get away from the reality that the punitive or disciplinary actions of good parents have the

---

[29] Jonathan, *Grace Beyond the Grave*, 110; see also Gully, P., and Mulholland, J., *If Grace is True*, San Francisco, Harper Collins, 2003, 58.

objective of their child's ultimate good.[30] There has to be a reason for the discipline beyond "punishment for punishment's sake". I believe that this point is also central in understanding the justice of God.

Maybe the most awe-inspiring and wonderful illustration that Jesus provides us of God as a loving father is found in Luke 15. The chapter commences with the tax collectors and "sinners" gathered around to hear Jesus. This irritates the religious leaders who complain that Jesus welcomes sinners and eats with them. Following this accusation, Jesus tells three parables in quick succession. Firstly, Jesus compares God to the good shepherd who pursues the one sheep that is lost *"until he finds it"* (Lk. 15:4, my italics). This picture portrays God determinedly pur-suing the sinner until the point of repentance. Secondly, Jesus likens God to the woman who lost a silver coin. She sweeps the house and searches carefully *"until she finds it"* (Lk. 15:8, my italics). The lesson of this story is just like the first: when that which was lost is found, there is great rejoicing, as there will be great rejoicing in heaven over the one sinner who repents. Thirdly, Jesus tells the story of the lost, or prodigal, son (Lk. 15:11-31) which is perhaps the most direct and challenging of the three stories, with the prodigal's father graphically depicting Father God, whose broken heart was healed when he saw his son in the distance — "But while he was still a long way off, his father saw him and was filled with compassion for him; he ran to his son, threw his arms around him and kissed him" (Lk. 15:20). As with the parables of the lost sheep and the lost coin, a celebration ensued as the son who was lost is now found.

Throughout the years at Tamworth Elim Church, I have not tired of using this story to remind our church family of how the Son of God illustrated what his Father was like, to encourage a deeper love and appreciation of God's character, and to correct some mistaken views.

Let us not forget, either, that God's love isn't some fickle, inconsistent, vacillating, unpredictable love of a fallible human being, but it is an eternal and enduring love, indestructible and unyielding. Paul writes, "For I am convinced that neither death nor life, neither angels nor demons, neither the present nor the future, nor any powers, neither height nor depth, nor anything else in all creation, will be able to separate us from the love of God that is in Christ Jesus our Lord" (Rom. 8:38-39).

---

[30] Jonathan, *Grace Beyond the Grave*, 111.

One of our most used maxims at Tamworth Elim is borrowed from author Philip Yancey's *What's So Amazing About Grace?* This is a book I find to be quite awe-inspiring and it remains one of the most stimulating Christian books I have ever read. I just kept seeing examples of grace all around me in a multitude of ways after reading this book.

Yancey summarised God's grace into a memorable sentence: "Grace means there is nothing I can do to make God love me more, and nothing I can do to make God love me less."[31] This one sentence has been repeated many times since I preached a series on God's grace in 1998, through countless sermons and personal conversations, and is a saying that has caught the imagination of our church family. Right at the heart of all we do there lies this wonderful truth that God's love isn't purchased through our good deeds or through religious or charitable actions; it is totally and wonderfully undeserved. In over twenty years, that one amazing truth has acted as a motivation *par excellence* to our church family, for when one truly understands the magnificence of God's love, it changes everything — the way we look at God, at ourselves and at the world around us. We begin to see others through grace-healed eyes and appreciate their potential. For they, like us, are recipients of the grace that God so lavishly bestowed, a love that was directed to them, and us, while they (we) were still sinners.

American pastor/theologian J. D. Greear asserts that Jesus' death has fully paid for every ounce of our sin and his perfect life has been credited to our account. In fact, "Christ's obedience is so spectacular there is nothing we could ever add to it, and his death so final that there is nothing that we could ever take away from it."[32] That is why the writer to Hebrews tells us that we do not come into the presence of God timidly or apprehensively, but with boldness.

How do you think God feels about you right now? Please try not to blurt out some platitude but think carefully about your answer. Okay. How did you determine your answer? Did you base your answer on the kind of week that you've just had? Maybe, spiritually-speaking, you feel

[31] Yancey, P., *What's So Amazing About Grace?* Grand Rapids, Zondervan Publishing House, 1997, 71.
[32] Greear, J. D., *Gospel: Recovering the Power that Made Christianity Revolutionary,* Nashville: B&H Publishing Group, 2011, 48.

you had a good week. Perhaps you've managed times of prayer and Bible study most days, you've been nice to your kids and have not given in to temptation in any way. Furthermore, this week you might have witnessed to that friend at work, refrained from kicking the cat, and you did not swear at that boy racer who nearly caused an accident. Well done for being such an amazing example of humanity! But that doesn't make you more righteous or loved by God.

Maybe the opposite is true. Maybe you feel pretty distant from God today because you've not even managed to say hello to God, let alone have special "quiet times" in his presence. Maybe you've fallen into temptation on the internet — you've gone surfing in dangerous waters enjoying the excitement of the moment, but you've despised yourself since. Perhaps you're feeling downcast today because you treated your loved ones with contempt or because of the way that you've missed opportunities to speak up for Jesus? Maybe you tarnished your Christian witness through some "unchristian" action or reaction *etc.* I'm sure that most of us have fallen foul to that kind of works-based thinking from time to time. But are we right in thinking this way?

Let's come back to Yancey's amazing summary of grace: "Grace means there is nothing I can do to make God love me more, and nothing I can do to make God love me less." When you think about his words, they make perfect sense. Let's reason this out together. Firstly, God's love is perfect. No believer is going to disagree with that! Therefore, if his love is perfect, it cannot be improved upon or enhanced or upgraded. The reason he loves us perfectly is because he is not merely a God who loves, he *is* love. He is the epitome of love, he defines love and he sets the standard on what love is.

So, if we do something good — if we read our Bibles every day for the next year, pray three hours every day before work, give away 50% of our wealth to serve the purposes of his kingdom and lead twenty people to Jesus before the end of the month — he cannot love us any more than he does right now. Why? Because his love for us is already perfect. Perfect is perfect! It is absolute, and to propose that God would love us more would suggest that his love wasn't perfect in the first place.

I'm not finished yet. If he were to love us less because we have done something to upset him — not read our Bible for ten days, or not prayed for three weeks, or worse — then he would be fickle and changeable. His love would be conditional, not unconditional; it would be merited, not unmerited. So that is why I love Yancey's great statement so much. To encourage a church to move away from a works-based way of thinking into a grace-filled mindset and lifestyle doesn't happen overnight, but I would encourage pastors to keep teaching, preaching, encouraging and exhorting their congregations on the subject of God's amazing grace. It's life-changing! The impact on our lives and on the people we have contact with will be significant.

Just be aware that this is not an easy road to travel, especially if your church has been fed a diet of works-based acceptance for many years. To some it will sound like a different, questionable and very suspect "gospel". You might even get accused of giving Christian people licence to live immorally or sinfully. That was the very thing that St. Paul was accused of when he taught about grace! In his magnificent letter to the Romans, he anticipates an objection to grace and raises a hypothetical argument from a grace protestor: "What shall we say, then? Shall we go on sinning, so that grace may increase? By no means! We died to sin; how can we live in it any longer? ... What then? Shall we sin because we are not under law but under grace? By no means!" (Rom. 6:1-2,15).

I love the J. B. Phillips translation of this passage. Phillips was a very English, pipe-smoking Anglican clergyman and scholar. He writes, "Now what is our response to be? Shall we sin to our heart's content and see how far we can go to exploit the grace of God? What a ghastly thought! ... Shall we go on sinning because we have no Law to condemn us anymore, but are living under grace? Never!"[33] I chuckle to myself every time I read his translation. In my imagination, I can hear Phillips, an Oxbridge academic in Classics and English, saying in rather pompous tones the words, "What a ghastly thought!" It was the pastor of Westminster Chapel, D. Martyn Lloyd Jones, who once said, "If your preaching of the gospel of God's free grace in Jesus Christ does not provoke the charge from some of antinomianism, you're not preaching the gospel of the free grace of God in Jesus Christ." Food for thought, I think!

Grace is distinctive to the Christian religion. Yancey tells of the great scholar C. S. Lewis attending a British conference on comparative religions, with experts from around the world debating what, if any, belief was unique to Christianity. The group discussed many possibilities until Lewis entered the room. Lewis asked what the rumpus was all about. He was told that they were discussing Christianity's unique

---

[33] Phillips, J. B., *Letters to Young Churches,* Macmillan, 1948.

contribution to world religions. Lewis responded, "Oh, that's easy. It's grace!" Yancey writes, "After some discussion, the conference had to agree. The notion of God's love coming to us free of charge, no strings attached, seems to go against every instinct of humanity. The Buddhist eight-fold path, the Hindu doctrine of karma, the Jewish covenant and the Muslim code of law — each of these offers a way to earn approval. Only Christianity dares to make God's love unconditional."[34]

Both Old and New Testaments are full of stories of grace. There are narratives like Saul's disabled grandson Mephibosheth being welcomed into King David's household and given a seat at the king's table, even though he did nothing to deserve it (2 Sam. 9:1-13), and the story of Jonah, who was given a message from God to take to the wicked Ninevites — a message that ultimately brought repentance and restoration. Jonah anticipated that God was going to "go easy" on this malevolent people group and disagreed unequivocally with such benevolence. He believed the Ninevites should be punished for their sins. This OT book depicts the grace of God in stark contrast to the lack of grace of weasel-like Jonah. Sadly, such a deficiency of grace, on occasions, is witnessed in the reactions and behaviour of Christians — you and me — who stand out like a sore thumb in contrast to the God we claim to worship and follow.

Examples of God's amazing grace are to be found on virtually every page of the New Testament, especially through the life, ministry and teaching of Jesus. The grace of Christ is evident in his attitude and responses to the undeserving, those on the margins of society and those who were despised by many holier-than-thou religious leaders. Jesus also emphasised grace through his teachings and parables. He taught his followers to go the second mile, to turn the other cheek, to love their enemies and to forgive a person not seven times, as Peter suggested, but seventy-seven times.[35] Jesus never taught anything that he did not practise himself. Think no further than his prayer on the cross, asking for Father God to forgive those who did not know what they were doing in crucifying him.

Furthermore, many of his parables accentuated grace. The prodigal son was treated far better by his father than his selfish and sinful ways deserved. People on the highways and byways of life, both good and bad,

---

[34] Yancey, *What's So Amazing About Grace?* 45.
[35] Or "seventy times seven" in some manuscripts.

were invited to the wedding banquet. The Good Samaritan responded to a Jew with compassion and mercy, which is astounding as Jews and Samaritans had nothing to do with each other socially. Then there was a tax collector who prayed alongside a self-righteous Pharisee. Jesus' punchline in telling this story was that the humble will be exalted. Grace, grace, grace!

One of the greatest examples of God's amazing grace is found in the Apostle Paul. He wrote to the church at Corinth and declared, "For I am the least of the apostles and do not even deserve to be called an apostle, because I persecuted the church of God. But by the grace of God I am what I am, and his grace to me was not without effect. No, I worked harder than all of them — yet not I, but the grace of God that was with me" (1 Cor. 15:9-10).

Religion says, "I obey; therefore, I am accepted by God," but the gospel of grace says, "I am accepted by God, through Christ, therefore I obey."[36] Religion can tell you to love God with all your heart and your neighbour as yourself, but only the gospel gives you power to do it. In the earlier part of Paul's life — when he was known as Saul of Tarsus — he was zealous for the Law, a zeal that brought him into confrontation with every group or person that he regarded as a threat. Paul not only kept the minute details of his Jewish religion, but he went out of his way to rid the earth of every enemy to his religion, and there were no greater enemies than followers of Christ. He was a zealot in his following the God of Abraham, Isaac and Jacob. A modern-day example would be ISIS, for they not only desire to follow the Koran and embrace Sharia Law, but they zealously desire to wipe the earth of infidels (those who are not followers of the teachings of the Prophet Mohammed).

Furthermore, Paul formerly believed that his religious observance and spiritual pedigree as a practising Jew gained him credit with God,[37] but later came to believe that all this was quite useless. Paul writes to the Philippian church, listing what he had formerly thought were his spiritual credentials, then asserts, "I consider everything a loss compared to the surpassing greatness of knowing Christ Jesus my Lord, for whose sake I have lost all things. I consider them rubbish that I may gain Christ..."

---

[36] Timothy Keller in Greear, J. D., *Gospel: Recovering the Power that Made Christianity Revolutionary,* Nashville: B&H Publishing Group, 2011, xiv.

[37] See Philippians 3 for an insight into the way that Paul viewed himself before and after his encounter on the Damascus road.

(Phil. 3:8). Basically, he is saying that all those things that he thought were advantageous in getting him closer to God he now considers "rubbish". The Greek word that the NIV very politely translated as "rubbish" is actually much stronger than that. It essentially means dung, but even now I may be putting it a little more respectfully than Paul did!

As I say, for me, it all starts with God, a God who is not merely loving but One who defines himself as love. When we grasp this awesome truth, it will affect everything and will transform the way that we look at ourselves, other people, life, faith and God himself, because, "Grace means there is nothing I can do to make God love me more, and nothing I can do to make God love me less."

Father God,

The magnitude of your love for your world, despite all its flaws, rebellion and ugliness, is beyond description or comprehension. To be recipients of your unyielding compassion is as humbling as it is exhilarating.

As we continue on our daily walk with you, please give us a better, healthy understanding of who you are. Whilst we bask in the comfort of your love, we also recognise that your heart breaks when we stray away from your purposes for our lives, and we ask for your forgiveness for the many times we have failed you. May we never intentionally grieve you, Lord, but instead, with the help of the Holy Spirit, let us be diligent in pursuing your perfect will and loving others as you have loved us.

Amen.

CHAPTER TWENTY-THREE

Acts 29

AS I WRITE, I REMAIN CONSCIOUS OF ALL THE STORIES, MIN-
istries and amazing people that I haven't mentioned at all. I actually feel
quite embarrassed by this. John concludes his Gospel, "Jesus did many
other things as well. If all of them were recorded, I imagine the world
itself wouldn't have enough room for the scrolls that would be written"
(Jn. 21:25). I hear a touch of exasperation in John's voice. John was, I
think, a little frustrated because there was so much more he wanted to
say. It is a similar frustration to what I feel as I come to the end of *Grace
and Glory*. What I have been able to share is only the tip of the tip of the
iceberg. Some great stories have simply slipped from my memory as I am
only human; others could not be shared, either because they are too
painful or because they draw other people unwillingly into the narrative
which would be unkind, unethical and unprofessional.

I have tried to be real, and not put a superficial or triumphalist gloss
on what I have written. My life has been a mixture of faith and doubt,
successes and failures, mountains and valleys, times when I found myself
believing for the impossible and other times when I questioned
everything. I hope that you find my transparency more of a help than a
hindrance.

Luke wrote two magnificent volumes, both included in our New
Testament. The first, Luke's Gospel, is an account of all that Jesus did
whilst on earth. Luke takes us from the birth narratives of Christ up to
his resurrection and ascension. His second volume, Acts, commences
with the ascension of Jesus and is an account of all that the risen Christ
achieved through the giving of the Holy Spirit. This volume takes us
through the expansion of the church, as believers were empowered to be
Christ's witnesses in Jerusalem, and throughout Judea, Samaria and then
to the ends of the earth. His inspiring, historical narrative concludes with

Paul getting to Rome and remaining under house arrest, awaiting trial by Caesar. Many scholars believe that Paul was released in AD 62.

But why did Luke need to stop with Paul under house arrest in Rome? Why couldn't there have been an Acts 29? Why didn't he tell us whether Paul actually went on a fourth missionary trip, and what ultimately happened to Paul? Was he really beheaded at the order of Roman Emperor Nero, as early church historian Eusebius claimed?

I suppose Luke finished with Paul in prison because he needed to finish somewhere. Sorry if that sounds a bit of a damp squib of an answer, but I am actually thankful that Luke didn't stop before he did. The reason that I have taken our narrative to this point is that I am now up-to-date. This book now needs to be published. This is where we've got to, but I also realise that there are many astonishing adventures yet to be written where God will undoubtedly fulfil many breathtaking acts among us, when I will no longer be serving in my present capacity, and where others will, in God, achieve far more than has been achieved under my leadership — please, God!

The narrative continues, but whatever the story that lies ahead, it will be all by his grace and ultimately all for his glory.

Dear Lord Jesus,

You are "the Alpha and Omega, the first and the last, the beginning and the end", and by your grace, at this appointed time, you have afforded us the privilege to be an infinitesimal, yet significant, part of your great story. Our time on Earth's stage is fleeting, but we pray that we will make our lives count in the extension of your kingdom.

We thank you for those who will come after us to play their parts as your story continues, and pray your blessing upon them. We live by your grace and everything we do is for your glory.

Amen.

"Expect great things from God
and attempt great things for God!"

— William Carey —

Contact the Authors

To contact the authors, please write to:

Stephen and Julie Jonathan
c/o Elim Church
Bamford Street
Glascote
Tamworth
B77 2AT

Or send an email to:

stephen.jonathan@tamworth-elim.org.uk
(We would love to hear from you.)

Or visit the church website for more information:

www.tamworth-elim.org.uk